JONES

Diary of an Undercover Psychopath

STEPHEN JAYDELL

Copyright © 2021 Stephen Jaydell

The British Crime Franchise.
Book 3

All rights reserved.
ISBN: 9798837309380

Disclaimer

While this book is based around real life events none of the characters or institutions portrayed are in any way based on real people or organisations, any similarity is purely coincidental. Although real people, places and organisations are referenced, they are intermingled with fictional facts and figures in order to dramatize the story.

FRIDAY 16th JANUARY 1981
1700 HOURS
METROPOLITAN POLICE TRAINING FACILITY, HENDON

My name is Andrew David Jones, Identification Number UX838. I'm 21-years old and a Cadet in Her Majesty's Metropolitan Police, been here for 8 months now, due to pass out in March. My team leader, John, thinks it's a good idea to write stuff like this down, get things off my chest, but I'm not too sure, feels a bit poncy to me. He's a good guy though, smart too, I'll do well to listen to him. God knows how often I'll write, I'm not the best at writing truth be told but I'll try and do it most days, maybe give myself the weekends off. I'm not writing no procedural shite neither, nah, life's too short for all that crap. John reckons I should keep it real, about me and how I'm feeling, reckons it'll help me control my emotions and all that fairy sounding bullshit. Yeah, we'll see.

Andy.

SUNDAY 18th JANUARY 1981
1800 HOURS
METROPOLITAN POLICE TRAINING
FACILITY, HENDON

Shit weekend, away at Brighton, got done one-nil. I couldn't go, nah, according to the gaffer it's not "appropriate" for a trainee copper so I got a couple of cans from the off-license and listened to it on the radio. Without a win in maybe four games, we're slipping down the table, which is shit. Had a curry with John last night, a few of us were supposed to go but they all cried off, (twats), so ends up just me and him. Think he might well be a fairy, not 100% sure but he sounds like one with a plumb in his mouth and all that. Next week we have "urban control" training, riot drill to you and me, yeah, I'm looking forward to that. Then, week after, I'll be on work experience. Been posted to Lambeth division, it's alright I suppose, better than down my way over in Canning Town, nah, bumping into my old mates, catching them on the chore would be shit, but funny though. Sergeant Smith is on at me to be more consistent, reckons I'm a good lad and will become a decent officer, says he wants me to leave my past behind and start thinking like a copper.

Andy.

THURSDAY 22nd JANUARY 1981
LATE, FUCK KNOWS THE TIME
AT HOME, NEW PARK AVENUE, EDMONTON

Today's been the best day. Just got back from a tasty Indian with the lads, had fuck-knows how many pints plus a few Pernod and Blacks, so I'm a bit worse for wear if I'm honest. Not sure I should be writing this pissed-up, but I'll forget in the morning. We did the riot drill today in the shell-city, yeah, out the back of Hendon there's a make-believe street with shell-houses where we practice front line work. Soon as we get there, we see a fucking Cortina on it's side burning to fuck, and a load of Month-1 cadets giving it large, pretending to be a rioting mob, like what I did when I first joined up. Plastic shields handed out, we're told to go disperse them, turns out to be the best fun ever. John, calling the shots, had us working as a team, me and Donnie are giving what-for, pushing and shoving the dickheads and giving them verbal's, the fucking clueless twats. Not to worry, it'll be their turn in a few months where they can give it back. Fuck me, the worlds spinning, I'm so pissed, pissed as a fart, fucking hell. Saturday and Sunday I'm at Brixton Station for work experience, feels a bit weird down there with all those ethnic types, can I say that, fuck it, yeah I can. The gaffer says I got to be careful with my language and what I write down, says poncy lawyers will read everything out in court and I'll look like a twat.
Like I care.

Jonesy.

**FRIDAY 23rd JANUARY 1981
1410 HOURS
METROPOLITAN POLICE TRAINING
FACILITY, HENDON**

Off to the Frontline tomorrow so finished early today. The team have been taking the piss, but I'm not worried, it's the locals who call it the frontline, like they're at war with us, which they aren't, we're there to stop them robbing and killing each other, the fucking idiots. Had a run in today with Donnie fucking MacDougal, the Scottish twat, he can take his kilt and shove it up his fat Glaswegian arse. Larging it in the shower, he's going on about "barrow-boys" and "pie-n-mash", trying to wind me up, but he can fucking do one, I'll crush his haggis-shaped head if he tries it on.

Andy.

SATURDAY 24th JANUARY 1981
2145 HOURS
TOILET BLOCK, BRIXTON POLICE STATION

Been assigned to a pair of older C.I.D. guys, fuck me, they're boring. Higgston looks to be coasting till retirement in a year or so, and Collins is an old school dirt-bag, probably on the game, the fuckin old codger. Rumour is he's got a few informants on the go and is well known around the Frontline as a wrong-un. Shift starts at 2200-hours so just taking a quick dump, thought I better get some diary in now. Got the tube down here earlier, fuck me, it's urban alright, not as bad as the chaps back at Hendon were saying though. Soon as I come out of the station, I hear reggae music and eye loads of them down the market buying yams and green bananas, to be fair, they look to be keeping themselves to themselves. Don't know what we're doing tonight, just basic patrol I think. Got Man United in the week, can't wait.

Andy.

SUNDAY 25th JANUARY 1981
2145 HOURS
TUBE TRAIN, JUST PAST BAKER STREET

Not sure I'm cut out to be a copper. Totally embarrassed myself today, no doubt the gaffer up at Hendon will get to hear about it. On foot patrol, along with Higgston, both in plain cloths, which is pretty cool to be fair, we see a couple of little shits looking shifty. Intending to execute a Section 4, as procedure, we separate them and I notice my suspect acting very suspiciously, reacting in a hostile manner. I got no choice but to use force to restrain him, which is seen by a passer-by who starts shouting hysterics, the fucking slag. Arriving in an unmarked car, (too fat and lazy to walk, the cunt), Collins takes over the search, eventually letting both suspects go with a stern warning before reprimanding me for using excessive force. Me, excessive force, what about the fucking little shit giving it large. He'll no doubt ring Smithy at Hendon in the morning and I'll be up for a bollocking.
Just what I need.

Andrew Jones.

WEDNESDAY 28th JANUARY 1981
1800 HOURS
AT HOME, NEW PARK AVENUE, EDMONTON

Can't wait to pass out, get out and do some real police work. Sargeant Smith pulled me yesterday to give me a Section 12. The triplicate form says "inappropriate use of language", which is a touch, yeah, if excessive force was mentioned I'd be fucked. Smithy says it'll stay on my record for 12 months, and, if I get another during that time, it'll see me kicked out. Serious shit. John reckons I should think about what makes me feel angry or frustrated, then write that shit down. Yeah, understanding it is the first step in controlling it, apparently. All this has got me thinking whether I'm really cut out for the police. Sure, my mum and dad are proud, but, if I'm honest, me in uniform just feels wrong sometimes. Back in the day, the force was a real "force", keeping us tearaways in check with a quick clip around the ear, yeah, that'll do it, worked for me. Nowadays, fuck me, we've got to be all formal, documenting everything, the paperwork drives me mad. Petty theft, robbing stereos from cars or the odd punch up down at Upton Park aint crimes of the century, fuck me, me and my mates did way worse, part and parcel of growing up in inner-city London. Fuck me, suppose writing this shit down does help.

Andy.

SUNDAY 8th FEBRUARY 1981
1800 HOURS
AT HOME, NEW PARK AVENUE, EDMONTON

Just got a call from my old man, telling me my cousin Kenneth's been arrested. Can't believe it, he's done really well for himself landing a job in the City buying and selling commodities or something. Turns out his flat got raided in the early hours and he's found with a decent amount of cocaine and a gun, with ammunition. He's awaiting a court appearance tomorrow. Fuck knows how or why he's got drugs, or a firearm for that matter when he's a professional guy, the bloody idiot. The old man's asked if I can pull any strings, which of course I can't. I should probably tell Smithy though, just in case there's any come back to me. Yeah, I'll pop into his office tomorrow when I head back to Hendon.

Andy.

TUESDAY 10th FEBRUARY 1981
1030 HOURS
METROPOLITAN POLICE TRAINING
FACILITY, HENDON

Told Smithy about my cousin, says it doesn't matter but he'll make a formal note, just in case. Reckons I should keep my distance, steer clear of any potentially conflicting situations. Sounds like good advice. Confiding in John, I tell him what's happened, he's become a bit of a mate I suppose. Thinks, worst case, he could get up to 20-years, which is madness, but it all depends on the Judge. I'll not tell the old man, he'll get stressed and his angina will play up again. Anyhow, I got 2 weeks or thereabouts until passing out, between now and then, I got 2 physicals, which will be a doddle, and 3 written exams, which I'll struggle with. Still, things are looking up, we got Coventry at home today in the Cup, should be on for a win. Reckon we're on for promotion this season, unless we fuck it up, which we probably will.

Andy.

MONDAY 16th FEBRUARY 1981
2000 HOURS
AT HOME, NEW PARK AVENUE, EDMONTON

Just back from work and she's fucking on at me already about sorting out the garden fence and cutting the grass blah-blah-blah. Message from my old man though, Kenny's been remanded, due for trial end of May. I'll go see him in a few weeks, yeah, he'll be okay, he's tough, could always handle himself down the boxing club. A few years older than me but surprising fast for a big lad, my old man reckons he could have had a decent fight career as a pro, probably at national level, european maybe. His job in the City will be fucked though, can't imagine they'll take too well to a convicted criminal, we'll have to wait and see. After a few weeks off, I'm back down at Brixton later in the week, hopefully I won't make another pratt of myself, I know I have to control my temper and play the long game. With an exam tomorrow, I got some books from John to scan through after tea. Wonder what shit she's burnt for us today, hope it's better than yesterdays incinerated toad-in-the-hole crap.

Andy.

TUESDAY 17th FEBRUARY 1981
0700 HOURS
AT HOME, NEW PARK AVENUE, EDMONTON

Massive row last light with Janice, fucking moody cow. I'm wanting to get the books out for some revision but she's rabbiting on and on and fucking on, chatting complete bullshit after bullshit after fucking bullshit. I fucking hate her. Plus, on top of all this, some cunt's tried to blow the Pope up in India or Pakistan or somewhere the fuck, the set of twats. I'm not one bit religious but, fucking hell, that's not on. Just what I need before an exam today. Perfect.

Andy.

**FRIDAY 20th FEBRUARY 1981
1400 HOURS
METROPOLITAN POLICE TRAINING
FACILITY, HENDON**

Been clearing out my locker, yeah, tomorrow is "passing out" day. Thankfully, I've passed everything I need to, which is a relief, yeah, never been bright or clever, I got exams in woodwork, P.E. and maths, but hated school and the idiot teachers, fellow students too. I tended to hang around with kids way older than me, Kenny's mates and all that lot. Fuck it, the past is the past and I'm bloody chuffed to be passing out, who'd have thought it. In the locker room everyone's giddy excited about tomorrow, too right, apart from a good piss up, we formally graduate and find out what our official postings are. You know what, I'll miss the chaps, but never admit it to them, good guys really, even if Donnie is a Scottish twat. I'll miss John the most, he's a good guy, sensitive I suppose, but still tough, super smart too. Everyone thinks he'll be posted to the Yard in some high-flying desk-bound job. That's not me though, nah, I want to me out there on the beat, doing proper policing. A bit of a tear-away when I was younger, never for one minute did I think I might end up being a copper. Mum and dad will be proud, she's bought a new dress and he's dusted off his old suit. It'll be a good day.

Jonesy.

SUNDAY 22nd FEBRUARY 1981
1320 HOURS
AT HOME, NEW PARK AVENUE, EDMONTON

Fuck me, hangover from hell. Passing out was hilarious though. Donnie makes a pass at Johns old dear, who, by the way, is a tasty bit of skirt, for an old bird. You know what though, she looks like she was up for a bit of Haggis, all flirty and smiles and revealing tops. John wasn't too happy with him, or her, looked embarrassed bless him. The ceremony itself was okay I suppose, a bit long, but mum and dad were incredibly proud. You know what, I'm going to make a success of this, build a life, make them even more proud. Janice, well, she was Janice, sitting around all day with a face like a smacked arse, the moody fat cow. Things got lively when we got back to the pub though, what a night. Pissed-up on gin and orange, she ends up sucking me off in the hallway soon as we get home. John and his old dear slipped away early on, I didn't really expect him to stick around, he never does. He's been posted to Lambeth Division, like I have, but he's in headquarters whereas I've been posted to the fucking frontline, yeah, back to Brixton nick. I'll have to learn how to speak patois now, might have to get into reggae too. Funny. Heading down there tomorrow for a look-round, meet the new Sarge and pick my uniform up.

Andy.

MONDAY 23rd FEBRUARY 1981
2330 HOURS
AT HOME, NEW PARK AVENUE, EDMONTON

First day done, not too bad. As a newbie, I thought the old-school coppers might take the piss but they're all pretty supportive actually. Journey down there isn't too bad either, train to Seven Sisters then tube all the way. My old man reckoned me moving out to Edmonton was a mistake, out of the East End and miles away but I can't grumble, it's a nice house with a front and back garden. Not sure I can do this diary thing for a while though, so much to take in with the new job, my time at Hendon didn't really prepare me for all the paperwork. Still, exciting times.

Andy.

SUNDAY 22nd MARCH 1981
0815 HOURS
AT HOME, NEW PARK AVENUE, EDMONTON

Shit, been a month since I last wrote. Feel like a proper copper now, yeah, made my first arrest a few weeks ago, hasn't let up since, mainly public order offences, disturbing the peace or street dealing, nothing too serious. Couple of weeks back, I had to give chase to a dickhead punk robbing a little old dear, bless her. Had it on his toes lively, in and out of Angel Town, (the Loughborough Estate to me and you), eventually, I caught the cunt. Unfortunately, (wink-wink), while apprehending him he managed to slip and bang his head, ended up with a cut to his forehead, a suspected broken nose plus a lovely shiner, even if I say so myself. The fucking little shit will think twice about mugging little old ladies now.

Andy.

FRIDAY 3rd APRIL 1981
2235 HOURS
BRIXTON POLICE STATION

Refs for half an hour, thought I'd write some notes while I take a shit. Hate the late shift, even more on a weekend, but, to be fair, it's pretty shit around here no matter what time or day. The locals come alive at the weekend, smoking weed and drinking beer, yeah, boisterousness and drug dealing tends to increase on Friday and Saturday nights. Last weekend for example, I stop a guy coming out of his car, he's weaving across the road, mounting the curb while parking, yet, I get no end of abuse from the dickhead. They fucking hate us, in fact, they hate any form of authority. It's not just the ethnics neither, nah, I had a domestic to deal with earlier. A thick-as-fuck paddy gets paid at midday and has been in the pub all afternoon gambling half of it away and pissing the other half up the wall. Stumbling home later, the missus gives him an earful, ends up with him knocking her around. We turn up and he's yelling crap about "carrots and parsnips" while taking wild swings at me. Using reasonable force to restrain him, (your honour), the dozy cunt gets a gashed head, so I've got no end of paperwork to deal with now. Some good news, new stop-and-search powers are defo coming in, about fucking time too, hopefully we can get a grip on all this.

Andy.

SATURDAY 4th APRIL 1981
0950 HOURS
AT HOME, NEW PARK AVENUE, EDMONTON

It's official, the higher-uppers have given "Red" approval for a new deployment called SWAMP '81, everyone's talking about it down the Station. Apparently, we're all being drafted into plain clothes, supported by the Special Patrol Group nutters, then, using informants, we've been instructed to nick as many wrong-uns as possible. A couple of portakabins have been drafted into the car park at the back of the Station to be used as temporary cells, Peckham and Walworth nicks are on standby too. We're to stop-and-search as many of them as possible, making sure we do this in a "highly visible" manner, which doesn't really make sense as we're in plain clothes. All this is going to go down like a lead-balloon with the locals, fuck me, they're going to go mental with this shit. You know what though, I don't care as long as I get a tonne of overtime out of it. Yeah, need the money see, Janice, the moany fat cow, has been on at me again about a fucking holiday to costa-lotta or wherever the fuck god knows where in Spain. Good news, Johns been appointed coordinator for the SWAMP 81 Operations Team, yeah, that's ace news, I'll tip him the wink, maybe he can sort me out some additional hours.

Andy.

THURSDAY 9th APRIL 1981
1710 HOURS
BRIXTON POLICE STATION

Dinner time. Fuck me, do I need it, this SWAMP bullshit is madness. I've stop-and-searched scores of locals, and, other than giving me a load of verbal's, most of them are 100% clean. Sure, a few have the odd spliff-worth of weed but none have any hard drugs or even offensive weapons. Still, even with a single spliff, they're nicked. The paperwork is a pain in the arse though, we have to record who we've stopped, where and when, why we've suspected them and all that bullshit. The tally sheet up in the custody suite shows something like 700 arrests, in less than a week. Of these, I bet no more than 30 will ever get to court and of these, probably only half will do any time at all, so why the fuck bother. I heard the higher-uppers want us to do even more sus-stops, house searches too. Rumour is the IRA are planning something big and all this swamp-shit is a smokescreen. I aint no fucking cannon-fodder pleb, they want to get the military involved yeah, get the squaddies down here tooled up, that'll sort them all out. Oh yeah, fucking Liverpool knocked us out of the cup last week, although we did beat Bristol in the league last game. If we win the Division, I'm defo getting a tattoo. The lads on the job say anything on my forearm will be frowned on, so it'll be on my leg or my back. Come on you hammers!

Jonesy.

**FRIDAY 10th APRIL 1981
MIDNIGHT HOURS
BRIXTON POLICE STATION**

Fucking nightmare this week, tonight's gone and topped it off nicely. Receiving reports of a gang fight at the tube station, we race around there pronto. The place is literally steaming full of ethnic youths, yelling and screaming, jostling and being rowdy. Turns out a young chap got himself stabbed then, when uniformed colleagues came to his aid, the idiot locals turn on them, pelting them with stones and bottles, the diabolical scum bags. Around a hundred of them gather on Atlantic Road, refusing to move on, the cheeky bastards until SPG units had it lively and showed them who's boss, dispersing them double-quick. The young guy's stable in hospital and the locals seem to have fucked off, however, we've all been told we can't clock off just yet, we've got to stay here on standby in case it all kicks off again. Giving Janice a call to let her know what's going on, she goes off on one saying this is all crap, that I'm knocking off some kind of slag down these sides. Charming. Anyway, chance would be a fine thing.

Jonesy.

SUNDAY 12th APRIL 1981
1835 HOURS
AT HOME, NEW PARK AVENUE, EDMONTON

Just got back, thank fuck, it all kicked off last night. Friday night was bad enough, but shit, last night was horrendous. After a late one on Friday, then the whole day on shift yesterday, we're told to increase the sus-stops even more. A few in the locker room reckon this is madness, bordering on harassment, sure to inflame the already shitty feeling down here. Anyhow, out on patrol, we see this dodgy fuck coming out of a taxi office about to get into a piece of shit rusty to fuck motor with no tax disc. Before I can say a word he starts swinging punches all over the place. Pretty handy to be honest, strong too, he could fight. Cuffs on, I drag him all over, clumping him left, right and centre. Claret everywhere, we hurl him into the back of a SPG wagon and a full scale inner city riot ensues. All along Railton Road the locals rip the place apart, finally fading away at around 0200-hours. Got sent home at midday, fucked, tiered and exhausted. Can't believe what's happened.

Andy.

MONDAY 13th APRIL 1981
1405 HOURS
BRIXTON POLICE STATION

Another shift, another day of revelation. The trouble on Saturday night made the front pages of all the newspapers plus the evening TV news reports too. We had the higher-uppers come visit the "scene" earlier, politicians too, (the twats!). Turns out, thousands of officers were drafted in from all over London although I didn't see any of this, nah, after the altercation at the taxi-office, I was deployed to a team controlling the "outer perimeter", near Herne Hill and Brockwell Park. Nothing more than glorified traffic work, it's tense with angry motorists giving it large, but the main action was down at Railton Road near the train station. Hundreds of officers got injured, a few taken to hospital with cuts and bruises, plus, turns out someone got shot at on Acre Lane. A couple of fire engines were attacked too resulting in the Windsor pub being burnt to the ground, no bad thing I reckon, it's well known as the epicentre of dealing on the Frontline. News reports suggest up to 500 youths were involved, but, talk back at the Station suggests it was closer to 2000, potentially many more if we hadn't of closed off the arterial routes.

Andrew.

WEDNESDAY 15th APRIL 1981
2340 HOURS
AT HOME, NEW PARK AVENUE, EDMONTON

Things are looking up. Got back tonight to find dinner made along with a bottle of wine. We had a good chat actually, with Janice crying, telling me how scared she was the other night listening to reports of the riot on the radio, knowing I was down there in the middle of it. We haven't been that close in ages, it was nice, I suppose. Even better, the evening ends up with us in bed and me pounding her red raw, yeah, loving it, she literally shook as she came. She's asleep now though, which is a shame, reckon I could go again to be fair. Felt good, we should do it more often, I should make more of an effort.

Andy, (super shagger!)

**THURSDAY 16th APRIL 1981
0800 HOURS
LAMBETH DIVISIONAL HEADQUARTERS,
COBALT SQUARE, VAUXHALL**

Heading up to Division today, I'm required to give a statement. Apparently, I was there when the trouble actually started so they intend to start their bullshit enquiry by speaking with me, maybe I'll get a medal or something. Don't quite know what to expect, although the gaffer is with me, Commander Crow, and my union rep too, a jumped-up grey-haired prick called Terry Paulson.

Andy.

THURSDAY 16th APRIL 1981
1115 HOURS
LAMBETH DIVISIONAL HEADQUARTERS, COBALT SQUARE, VAUXHALL

Fuck me, less a statement, more like an interrogation. Room full of higher-uppers, the bells-and-whistles-polished-buttoned dicks, plus a civilian chap chairing the session. They're quizzing me from all angles about the week leading up to the riot, the day in general and specifically the incident outside the taxi-office. The union guy turns out to be a legal genius, tells me a few times to make "no comment". Felt like I was on trial, like I was a suspect which is a bit fucking rich if you ask me, wasn't me tearing up my own street, kicking down garden walls and launching bricks at the police. Why the fuck am I on trial, the fucking shiny-shoed pricks.

PC Andrew Jones.

FRIDAY 17th APRIL 1981
1022 HOURS
AT HOME, NEW PARK AVENUE, EDMONTON

Brilliant news. Got a call this morning just before setting off saying I've been given the weekend off, to recuperate from the week I've had, and all the hassle I've been subjected to. Hassle, fuck off. Getting up at the crack of dawn for a day on a building site, driving a bus or doing the bins is hassle, worrying about paying the rent or feeding the kids, that's a hassle, fuck me, having a punch up with the locals and cracking some skulls is my idea of a good day out, hardly hassle. Anyhow, with the weekend off, I might go down the Orient tomorrow with the lads, should be a giggle.

Andy.

MONDAY 20th APRIL 1981
1022 HOURS
BRIXTON POLICE STATION

Got in this morning to find I've been assigned "light duties", sorting out the admin out in the custody suite. Fucking brilliant news, the Frontline can go fuck itself. Even better, we beat Orient 2-nill at the weekend, so we're defo promoted. Had a right laugh with the old gang at the weekend, went down to a shit-hole club in Deptford called "Cheeks", a mate of a mate does the doors apparently. The local slags love a bit of the East End down there, if you know what I mean, yeah, what goes on sarf-of-the-river, stays sarf!

Andy.

MONDAY 25th MAY 1981
1644 HOURS
BRIXTON POLICE STATION

Reading back, it's been a long while since I last wrote. To be honest, life's been pretty good, haven't felt the need to write anything down. I've been on light duties since the riot, bit of custody suite here, bit of admin in the C.I.D. office there. Spend most of my time tabulating the movements of a load of scumbag suspects, where they've been, who they've met, literally the cast of London's criminal underworld. West Ham were promoted as champions, yes, CHAMPIONS, winning 6 of our last 7 games. Can't wait for next season, we get to play at Arsenal, Tottenham, Liverpool, Man U and Leeds, back where we belong. So, reason for writing, just been told the higher-uppers want to see me tomorrow, 0900-hours at Divisional HQ. Fuck knows why, but I've called John, haven't seen or heard from him in ages, hoping he can shed some light.

Andy.

TUESDAY 26th MAY 1981
0924 HOURS
BRIXTON POLICE STATION

Turns out I've been re-assigned, yeah, as of Friday this week I'll be working West End Central, near Trafalgar Square. From what I can gather, it's mostly dealing with clueless tourists and office workers, either way, better than walking the streets on the Front-fucking-Line fearing for my life, literally hated by the people I'm there to help. Even better news, I'm not on light duties no more, nah, instead, I'll be doing actual police work. Get in, life just keeps getting better and better.

Jonesy.

SATURDAY 30th MAY 1981
0633 HOURS
CHARING CROSS POLICE STATION, AGAR STREET, LONDON

Just finished my first shift on the new job, absolutely ace, riding around in a pretty sweet Rover 3500 with a decent old-timer, Derek, likes to be known as "Rich Tea". This guy loves nothing more than reminiscing about the good old days over stewed tea and half a pack of biscuits. Our patch covers the majority of the West End, Trafalgar Square, Pall Mall and Piccadilly plus Soho, yeah, Soho, I love Soho. Touristy nowadays, bit of a cliché truth be told, but, down the back streets it's still teaming with Toms, some of them pretty tasty too. Old Rich likes a wave and a smile, but, to be honest, I wouldn't mind getting my cock wet in some of them, the dirty ole-bastard that I am.

Andy.

SUNDAY 31st MAY 1981
2355 HOURS
CHARING CROSS POLICE STATION, AGAR STREET, LONDON

The shift finishes at midnight but we're back in the Station for 2330, so, I've taken a quick shit. I'm really happy with this posting, no sign of any real trouble round these parts, yeah, a million miles from the "bomb-ber-clart" Frontline. Sure, we have a few alarm activations at shops here and there, some scuffles outside the pubs in Covent Garden and shoplifters in "Private" (sex) shops off Wardour Street, (who the fuck shop-lifts in a place like that?), but still, this is no Brixton, thank god.

Andy.

SUNDAY 12th JULY 1981
0207 HOURS
CHARING CROSS POLICE STATION, AGAR STREET, LONDON

Just knocked off, can't stop, but got to write this down. Earlier, got a shout to a gaff called Tylers Court, just off Wardour Street. Literally no more than meter wide, a dark and dingy narrow alley mid-way down on the right, there's a seedy "private" shop with blacked out windows and streamers over the door. Shout mentioned a "disturbance", turns out where some bloke received a "massage", (otherwise known as a hand-job), and is now dissatisfied, yeah, the dirty bastard's refusing to pay, it'd be funny if it wasn't so tragic. Talking to Maisey, the Tom, she says as soon as she touched him he went off like a machine gun, dropping his dirty load all over her, the poor cow. After us embarrassing him and the proprietor threatening to send a court summons to his house where his wife would see, he agrees to pay. Checking the Tom's okay, we get chatting and she asks if I'd like to walk her home after her shift finishes at 0300-hours, (surprised they actually have "shifts"). Too fucking right I do, she's a total sort and sexy as fuck. So, I'm off, hopefully for a nosh! When in Rome my son, when in Rome.

Andy (pandy).

SUNDAY 12th JULY 1981
1930 HOURS
AT HOME, NEW PARK AVENUE, EDMONTON

Bingo. Turns out, Maisey is the best fuck I've ever had. Energetic, physical, keen, eager, adventurous, she's fucking ace. Still, feel guilty about Janice and the vows I made a few years ago, they actually mean something to me. The old man and all my mates said we were too young to get married, but, I loved her, she loved me, plus, we were seeing each other since secondary school, so why not. Still, things have changed between us, we're distant and cold, the spark has sort of gone, I know she feels the same. Even on the rare occasion we do have sex, it's not right, it's awkward, forced, like it's a duty, not a pleasure. With Maisey though, it's most definitely a pleasure. I actually don't care she's a Tom, we all do shitty jobs, mine too. It's not who she is, it's just a job.

Andy.

MONDAY 23rd NOVEMBER 1981
1210 HOURS
CHARING CROSS POLICE STATION, AGAR STREET, LONDON

On the bog taking a long shit, just to waste some time. The summer's been steady, I love working here, yeah, the West End's a really good place to be a copper. Couple of weeks back, the old crew from Upton Park had a night out up West, the bastards, they knew I was on duty. So, they do what they do best and kick off at a pub in Leicester Square with a group of dirty Northerners, from Stoke I think. With reports of a "gang fight", I just know it's them. Chasing round there, I see it is indeed them, but, before I can turn around and do-one, they're goading the fuck out of me and taking the piss, the twats. I love the fellas though, proper mates, mates from school, they don't give a shit I'm a copper. Still seeing Maisey, she's so cool, she knows all about Janice, says she's okay with it all, says she understands how unhappy I am, says she's okay with me fucking other women too, can you believe that? Fair play to her.

Jonesy.

FRIDAY 27th NOVEMBER 1981
1850 HOURS
CHARING CROSS POLICE STATION, AGAR STREET, LONDON

Just about to go on shift. John was right you know, keeping a diary is good, reading some of it back helps me keep things in perspective. Having flicked through, I see I've noted a few choice events which, in the wrong hands, would be bad news at work and probably mean a divorce at home. I've started to keep this in the locker at work, probably the safest place. I'm not working with Rich Tea no more, nah, he's off to work with a new newbie cadet doing work experience, so I've been paired up with another guy called Peter, but everyone calls him "China" or "Bruce". Funny, but harsh. See, he's white but has a certain oriental look about him, yeah, ruler straight jet-black hair in a bowl-cut with slanty eyes spread wide across his face. He doesn't seem to mind though, seems to play up to it in fact. Not sure I like him, a bit strait-laced and up his own arse for my liking, not like Rich Tea who was laid back. The official report thing came out about the Brixton Riots, fuck me, everyone at the Station is talking about it. Says the riots were "spontaneous" and not pre-planned, (as some in the press suggested), and poverty played a large part. Nah, I'm not having that, that's complete bullshit, the locals just went wild. Nah, they didn't protest, it wasn't political, they just ripped the place apart and robbed all the shops. The report actually blames us for heavy handed policing, can you believe it. Fuck right off.

Andrew.

SATURDAY 12th DECEMBER 1981
0540 HOURS
CHARING CROSS POLICE STATION, AGAR STREET, LONDON

Turns out China's a top bloke, on the job for 12-years, he's pretty much seen it all. During a shout last night we sus-stopped three IC3 males, with a quarter of weed plus thirty-odd quid in cash on them. China pulls one of them to the side to question him, while, truncheon drawn, I keep my beady eye on the other two fucks. China comes back saying it's all sorted and they can go. What, why, I say. Shaking his head, he tips me a wink. Back in the motor, he hands me a tenner, says the suspect wanted to buy us a drink after work, for our trouble. So, as you can see, China is indeed a wrong-un, but, I'm actually okay with it. Those three fools would have probably got a discharge, so arresting them would have been a waste of everyone's time, especially ours.

Andy.

SATURDAY 2nd JANUARY 1982
1030 HOURS
CHARING CROSS POLICE STATION, AGAR STREET, LONDON

New Years Eve was immense. Sure, we had a lot of pissed up folk, some getting rowdy and a few muggers out on the rob, plus some gobby punks giving large over at Nelsons Column, but, the feel-good vibe was something else. Me and China have been pocketing a few shekels for ourselves as we go, some of the "private" shop keepers tip us a wink and buy us a drink for looking out for them. Plus, turns out me ole-China is partial to the odd spliff or two. Yeah, any time we confiscate any materials there's always a little less booked in than what we find on the suspects, he calls it the "angels" share, whereas I call it fairs-fair, what's mine is yours. Got to be careful though, ever since that shitty report was published last year about the riot, we've had lots of talks on how best to deal with suspects, stressing the need to write everything down. There's talk of new procedures being rushed through later in the year to better control all this, yeah, yet more fucking paperwork, just what we need. Me and Janice have been good recently, very good actually so, as a result, I haven't seen Maisey in a while. God, I do miss her tight little snatch and depraved sexual preferences though.

Yeah, all in all, all's good with Andy.

TUESDAY 19th JANUARY 1982
0810 HOURS
AT HOME, NEW PARK AVENUE, EDMONTON

Day off today, just as well. Had a blazing row with Janice last night, over a fucking TV show, the stupid fat cow. We got watching something about how the police investigate rape cases, fuck knows why, just something to watch. I'm pissing myself laughing as these clueless coppers get royally dicked in the arse by an undercover investigator, proving they don't take rape cases seriously enough. Even though I laughed, truth is it was shocking to see girls who've been raped aren't taken seriously, and pretty much get talked out of any case while the fucking idiot coppers stare at their tits. Don't get me wrong, you put yourself in a shitty position you got to expect you'll come out stinking of shit, but still, we're coppers yeah, so fucking do some coppering for fucks sake. Plus, these fucking small-dicked, clueless pricks who go around hitting birds, trying it on, forcing themselves onto them need stringing up. If I ever catch one, I'll give him a hiding as minimum for sure. You don't hit birds, full stop, it's like a man-code, you just don't do it, they are our wives, girlfriends and our mums for fucks sake. Anyway, Janice doesn't like my "dismissive attitude" whatever the fuck that means, so, we have a blazing row followed by fuck knows how long of not talking to each other. Perfect.

Andrew.

THURSDAY 21st JANUARY 1982
2300 HOURS
AT HOME, NEW PARK AVENUE, EDMONTON

Just got back. China pocketed a bullseye today from a shopkeeper on Meard Street, sorted me out a tenner for my trouble. I've told him to slow the fuck down, we're under the spotlight at the moment and fifty quid is a lot of dough, but, he's like a man possessed. I don't mind skimming a few quid here or there or the odd spliff now and again, but any sort of formalised protection racket bullshit and I'm out. Me and Janice still aren't talking, what a surprise, but fuck her, might go see Maisey. West Ham news, we've lost three on the bounce now, but doing alright in the league. Struggling for goals though, Goddard has 7, I think, and he's the top scorer. Not good enough.

Andy.

SATURDAY 23rd JANUARY 1982
0444 HOURS
AT HOME, NEW PARK AVENUE, EDMONTON

Saw Maisey last night, popped in while on patrol as China took a wander around Soho Square. Well happy to see me, we had a kiss and a cuddle then a quick nosh, which was just what I needed truth be told. Yeah, I arranged to meet her after the shift for more of the same. Walked her back to her place over at the Borough, smoked some joints courtesy of China and fucked for hours. Can't let Janice see my red-raw cock though, fuck me it's red, sore too.

Andy.

FRIDAY 29th JANUARY 1982
0655 HOURS
CHARING CROSS POLICE STATION, AGAR STREET, LONDON

Shit-shit-shit. Just popped to the bog to have a pre-shift shit and potentially a danger wank and noticed my cock is black, I'm not kidding, I've got a fucking black mamba in my pants!!! I aint really had a good look at it since the mammoth session with Maisey the other night, but, fucking hell, it's as black as the ace of spades, throbbing too. I hope I haven't caught a dose. Anyhow, China is indeed on the take, big time. Saw him yesterday pocket some cash from at least 2 shops, reckon he either packs that shit in when he's with me or, fucking cuts me in like proper partners. Yeah, could do with the extra cash to be fair, Janice is still on about going to Spain this summer, her sister's going, so, of course, she has to go too. Fucking hell.

Andy.

WEDNESDAY 10th FEBRUARY 1982
MIDDAY
CHARING CROSS POLICE STATION, AGAR STREET, LONDON

Worst day ever. Just seen a nurse over at St Thomas's Hospital. Still black as coal, I mentioned my "friends" cock to China, who reckons my "friend" should get it seen to sooner rather than later. Good advice. Went over in my civvies, could hardly go in uniform. Soon as I'm in the cubical explaining my predicament, the nurse who's about 30 or 40 and probably a bit of a looker in her day, starts smirking, struggling to contain the giggles. All matter of fact she tells me to drop my kegs and get the old fella out. I'm a big guy, 6-foot-6, reckon my shlong is as good as anyone's, so I whip him out pronto. Staring at it for a second or too, (I wondered if I might get a cheeky wank, but of course didn't), she asks me to pull my foreskin back. Quick once over, she tells me it's bruised, I've injured it in some way. Ah, see, I'm a copper, I say, got booted in the balls a week or so ago. Smiling, she nods, telling me it'll right itself in another week or so and to avoid "any more boots" before telling me to whip him back in then get dressed. Not a second too soon, felt like it might go off with her staring at it. Anyhow, good news it's not the clap, thank fuck.

Andy.

SUNDAY 21st FEBRUARY 1982
1037 HOURS
CHARING CROSS POLICE STATION, AGAR STREET, LONDON

Just been told I'm approaching my one-year anniversary as a fully uniformed copper. Shit, time has literally flown with the Riots, Rich Tea, Maisey and China, yeah, it's been a long year but gone really quickly. One of the Sergeants, a decent guy called Mike, suggested I should maybe consider the next step in my career. I've never thought of it as a career, just a decent steady job to be honest, yeah, I've been quite happy touring around the West End with China, doing our thing. We don't really talk about his business, other than him chucking me the odd tenner here and there. I really ought to try getting to know him a bit more, maybe broach the subject of becoming partners. The Hammers are playing like shit, yeah, after a strong start at the beginning of the season, since Christmas we've been pants. Lost away at fucking Southampton yesterday, shit game by all accounts. Not good.

Andy.

TUESDAY 16th MARCH 1982
1037 HOURS
AT HOME, NEW PARK AVENUE, EDMONTON

I must keep up with this diary lark, it's been a fucking age since I last picked it up. Anyhow, she's only gone and booked a 2-weeks package holiday for August, down on the Costa-Del-fuck-knows-where. That's the last thing I want to do with that boring old cunt, and, for 2-fucking weeks too. Other than that, things are ticking along just fine. Me and China have a good thing going on, my share is about a hundred quid a week from a few shop owners, plus a steady flow of dirty mags as and when I need them. China says what we're doing isn't necessarily illegal as there's no rules about us having other jobs, but it would probably be frowned on by the higher-uppers. Frowned upon, not fucking half! Got tomorrow off but haven't told Janice, instead, I'm spending the whole day with Maisey. Can't wait.

Andy.

THURSDAY 18th MARCH 1982
1745 HOURS
CHARING CROSS POLICE STATION, AGAR STREET, LONDON

Just got a bollocking. Yesterday, while I'm having an all-dayer with Maisey, China's out with a newbie cadet who sees him pocket some cash, then gobs off to one of the higher-uppers, the clueless piece of do-gooder dogshit. The Sarge gives China an official warning, and tells me in no uncertain terms, any more reports of back-handers or the like, I'll be up on a disciplinary. Fuck off, I'll be calling my union rep soon as I get home, that's nothing to do with me, that's fucking out of order. Better news, the day with Maisey was sweet, fuck me she's insatiable. Don't know too much about her though, she's guarded about her past, all she'll say is she's from up "up north", came down to London a few years back to get away from her over-bearing parents and perv-uncle. Their loss, my gain. I can't get enough of her, she excites me.

P.C. Andrew Jones.

SATURDAY 20th MARCH 1982
0230 HOURS
CHARING CROSS POLICE STATION, AGAR STREET, LONDON

Terrible news. Turns out, China's a fucking Yid, supporting Tottenham since he was a boy. Hasn't mentioned it until now because he knows I'm mad on West Ham, and we hammered them 4-nil at the beginning of the season. He's a gobby cunt though, not sure if I actually like him truth be told. In the canteen earlier, he's dropping hints about "perks of the job" and coppers getting "freebies" from Toms, clearly a dig at me and Maisey. I met the guy who looks after her today, Bev, (sounds like a girl's name, or at least a poofs name), "Bev-the-pleb", Maisey calls him. Older than me, he's as skinny as a rake, I'll fucking crush the cunt if it comes to it. So earlier, China confiscates some speed from a couple of Punk-Rockers on Trafalgar Square, asks if I want some. Smoking the odd spliff here and there is one thing, but proper drugs is something else. My mate Dex tried a "purple heart" when we were kids, made him trip out for best part of a week. China tells me speed's like being drunk, but without all the swaying and the urge to fight the world. You know what, I'm game if he is.

Andy.

SUNDAY 21st MARCH 1982
1030 HOURS
CHARING CROSS POLICE STATION, AGAR STREET, LONDON

Another late shift, which I like, means I can see Maisey after work and still be home when Janice, the lazy fat cow, wakes up in the morning. But, reason for writing is I'm sitting here on the shitter waiting to be disciplined. Yeah, earlier on, me and China dabbed some of that speed he got hold of, turns out, it's turbocharged madness, and I love it. We dabbed some of it back at the Station, then, thirty minutes later, we're driving around Soho Square when China drops a sly comment about Maisey. Slamming the brakes, I give him a bollocking and a slap for good measure. Affronted, jumping out the car he runs round my side, starts pulling at my door ranting and raving, giving it large. Before I realise what's happening, I'm out and chin the cunt. Turns out he's a pansy, can't take a punch, so crumbles like a sack of shit. Climbing back into the motor, he sits crying with his head in his hands while I'm in panic mode. I've just dropped a serving police officer, in the centre of London with fuck knows how many witnesses. Fuck knows what'll happen now.

Andy.

MONDAY 22nd MARCH 1982
1100 HOURS
AT HOME, NEW PARK AVENUE, EDMONTON

So, looks like I'm a lucky so and so and China is no grass. Yeah, so far, nobody, including China has made any complaint, so touch wood, I'm in the clear. He knows who's boss now though and I aint going to be dicked-around by no Yiddish ponce. The way I'm feeling right now, I'm taking over the business, yeah, he's the junior partner now and if he doesn't like it, he'll receive even more violence. More news, I had a call from an old colleague from Hendon, the Scottish twat called Donnie. Turns out, with the political situation with the Falkland Islands, looks like war's on the cards, so he's signed up and is ready to go. Not sure why he's bothering to call me, sure, part of the same team and all, but, at least from my part, we were never particularly mates, in fact, I always thought of him as a bit of a cunt actually. Anyhow, can't see a tin pot outfit like Argentina giving us any problems though, they're just arguing about fishing-rights or something.

Andy.

TUESDAY 6th APRIL 1982
2210 HOURS
AT HOME, NEW PARK AVENUE, EDMONTON

It's official, we're at war with Argentina, over the poxy Falkland Islands, literally a rock in the middle of the ocean, way over the other side of the world. We don't get anything productive from these lands, and, apparently, we only have a hundred or so English living there. Ask me, we have no right being down there anyway, we should ship everyone out and give the shithole back to the Argies. I suppose Donnie's on the first ship heading down there, yeah, always fond of an argument, the hard as nails Scottish twat will make a good squaddie I reckon.

Andy.

WEDNESDAY 7th APRIL 1982
MIDNIGHT
CHARING CROSS POLICE STATION, AGAR STREET, LONDON

On a refs break right now, it's really quiet tonight, other than a vigil by some hippie pricks in Trafalgar Square about the war. It's no war, it's Maggie wanting a victory under her belt so has picked a fight with the weakest of all opponents, classic bully-boy tactics. Had a call at home this morning, just before setting off. It was John, haven't heard from him in ages, told me about Donnie in case I hadn't heard, saying I should think about studying for the Sargeant exams, maybe look for a transfer to a Specialist Division. My arrest record is okay and solve-rate good too, so maybe something to think about. On a lighter note, West Ham beat the Wolves yesterday, decent 3-one win, we're doing well. Goddard got a brace, not bad for a bargain buy from QPR. Arranged to go out with the lads in a few weeks' time, away at the Gooners. Fucking hate Highbury, should be a good laugh though.

Andy.

SUNDAY 18th APRIL 1982
0450 HOURS
AT HOME, NEW PARK AVENUE, EDMONTON

What a night. Knocked off at midnight, got in 4-hours overtime which is great. After work, saw Maisey. Can't get enough of her, the sex is so much better than with Janice. She's telling me about the guy who looks after her, this Bev character. Officially, he rents her some "massage" space at the gaff on Tylers Court, but, in reality, he's her pimp. She says they used to be boyfriend and girlfriend but over time their relationship turned professional. Sounds like a cunt to me. Don't know what to do about China, he's bugging me big time, can't actually stand the fella, truth be told.

Andy.

SUNDAY 2nd MAY 1982
1230 HOURS
AT HOME, NEW PARK AVENUE, EDMONTON

Hangover from hell, had to call in sick today. Day off yesterday, met the old crew down at Canning Town, the George on Silvertown Way. All there, Dex, Will and Bee, fuck me, he stands out a mile off, and not just because he's black, nah, he's fucking massive, been weight training for about 9 months now, so he says. London derby so the pub opens early and by 1100-hours I've had three pints, by 1300, fuck knows how many. We get a cab to Highbury Fields then walk the rest of the way to their shithole. Losing 3-1, the lads are taking the piss, saying I'm a bad luck charm and we only ever lose when I'm watching. Outside, some fucking Gooner mug has a pop at Bee, but he drops the cocksucker like a sack of shit. A few others get involved and we end up fighting our way down Holloway Road. No police to be seen, just as well, I don't need that on my record. We finish up at the Bunker-Club, just off Shaftsbury Avenue. Dex introduces me to a top guy from the Millwall firm, who I thought would be trying to tear lumps out us, but, turns out the club is a well-known no-man's land, with an understanding there's no trouble to be had in there so that we can all enjoy a drink in peace. They call the Millwall chap "The Greek", turns out, he's actually alright, a decent guy. Vodka, spliffs and dabs of speed later, I end up back here with a fucking almighty headache at 0600-hours.

Andy.

TUESDAY 4th MAY 1982
2040 HOURS
AT HOME, NEW PARK AVENUE, EDMONTON

Made it home in record time today, only to find a Visiting Order from Kenny sitting on the doormat. As a serving officer, it doesn't look good me visiting a prisoner, but, he's family. I'll let one of the higher-uppers back at the Station know, just to cover me off, might actually check with the union rep too, yeah, that's smart thinking. Good news from the South Atlantic, we sunk an Argentine ship yesterday, fucking lovely!

Andy.

MONDAY 10th MAY 1982
1400 HOURS
AT HOME, NEW PARK AVENUE, EDMONTON

Just back from HMP Wormwood Scrubs, visiting Kenny. Fucking hell, if ever there was an advert to keep on the straight and narrow, it's that place. The imposing turrets and massive wooden gate at the front strike the fear of god into me, and I'm a super-hard streetwise bastard. Kenny's in a bad way though, truth be told. Bitter and twisted, he wants revenge on a couple of shysters who he reckons grassed him up and got him arrested. He's given me a few names to see if I can track them down, but, fuck that, I'm not getting into any of that business. He'll have to get his head down, do his time then come out a better man.

Andy.

**FRIDAY 14th MAY 1982
0730 HOURS
CHARING CROSS POLICE STATION, AGAR STREET, LONDON**

Just getting ready for roll-call, mate, I hate this shit. I'm on the early shift, tried to swap it to a late one because I want to see Maisey. As well as needing a good seeing to, I miss the dozy cow, can you believe it, me, having feelings for a fully paid-up Tom? Doesn't help that Janice is a fucking fat idiot, rabbiting on and fucking on about Spain. Will from the football has asked if he can come round tonight for a chat, fuck knows what about. I hope he or the others aren't in any trouble, needing me to pull some strings, nah, I've told them all to fuck that right off, Old-Bill or not, I aint getting into any of that. Anyhow, mustn't grumble, day off tomorrow, train up to the black country to face the Wolves, looking forward to that.

Andrew Jones.

FRIDAY 14th MAY 1982
2315 HOURS
AT HOME, NEW PARK AVENUE, EDMONTON

Fucking hell, Will can talk. Love him to bits, have done since primary school, but fuck me, he can gas. In the year above, along with Kenny, we all hung out together, Kenny and his mates, me and mine. Originally from Essex or somewhere, he moved to Mile End when he was 5, then came to our school aged 9 or 10. A wrong-un, or problem child, depending how you look at it, he's always in trouble, arguing with the teachers, giving them shit 24/7. Straight away though, he was a leader, sorting out teams for the mammoth football matches we'd have at lunch time, (Irish versus Italian versus England versus the Rest of the World / black kids), then what we'd all do after school. Nowadays, he has his own Scaffolding business and a lovely Mock-Tudor pad out near Billericay he shares with Sharn, a bird he met at school, (a bit too up herself for my liking), plus his two daughters. Over a cup of tea, he tells me tomorrows away game is likely to get a bit rough, with the Yam-Yam Army, (the Wolves bovver-boy gang, what a name by the way), threatening to do for us even before we get to their ground. Says he and the chaps will understand if I give it a miss. Bless him, but I aint missing this, no way. Nodding along, says he thought I'd say that, so asks me to keep an eye on some of the young-uns, be sure to tell them in our gang, "nobody runs, nobody hides", that's his motto. Bit nervous if I'm honest, but fuck it, I deserve a bit of fun and a laugh with the chaps.

Andy.

FRIDAY 21st MAY 1982
MIDNIGHT
CHARING CROSS POLICE STATION, AGAR STREET, LONDON

On a late shift, thank fuck, get to see Maisey later, yeah, get my balls sucked. Been off work Monday and Tuesday, well, to be fair, I was actually sent home on Monday. The Sarge says I can't police the streets of London with a shiner, if only he knew. The journey to the Wolves with the lads was a right laugh, just like old times. Their Ground, a twenty-minute walk through the town centre, a total shit-hole by the way, but we see no trouble, much to the disappointment of the fellas, maybe a dozen of us older chaps with around 30 young-uns. Mid-way through the game, we hear a rumour that a young-un has been attacked outside the ground, cut across his face. Losing 2-one, we decide to go sort this shit out. Fuck knows how he knew where to go, but Will leads us to their top-boys gaff, a short taxi-ride away. This guy, known as "Bollock-Head", (I kid you not), is a thick-as-shit bin-man, but, by all accounts, hard as fuck and the top boy of the Wolves "Yam-Yam" crew. We wait around the corner for a good couple of hours before he eventually comes home with a bag of chips. Following him inside we beat the living shit out of him as he scrambles into the kitchen where Bee smashes him over the head with a frying pan, (so funny!). Leaving him unconscious, we have it lively back to the train station. Somehow, I wake up on Sunday with a black eye and 2 days off work. Fun times!

Andy.

TUESDAY 1st JUNE 1982
0600 HOURS
AT HOME, NEW PARK AVENUE, EDMONTON

Getting ready for work, I've had to sit down, got a massive hangover. Bank Holiday yesterday, day off so spent it with Maisey. A lovely day, we walked through the West End up to Regents Park and the Zoo, never been there you know. Later on, back at hers, she suggests we take some speed, and have sex while high. Yeah, perfect. I've grown to love speed but fuck me, my cock nearly falls off. Orgasms while high are intense, so, while bucking into me she tells me to do her up the shitter. In for a penny, cucumber into a keyhole, it hurt like hell, felt as seedy as fuck, but, very sexy too. Then, when her door knocks we both stop and stare at each other. Who the fuck's that, I ask. Opening it, Bev's there, the fucking mug, looking around bollock naked me toward her. There you are you dirty slag, he shouts. Nah, I'm not having that, so nut the cunt. Falling back, he's on his knees, blood seeping through his fingers, tears in his eyes, he's shouting he'll dob me in. Fuck off, I kick the shit-cunt in the head before chucking him down the stairs. All the while, she's jumping on my back, shouting and yelling for me to stop-stop-stop, so she gets a slap too. Madness.

Andy.

WEDNESDAY 2nd JUNE 1982
0820 HOURS
CHARING CROSS POLICE STATION, AGAR STREET, LONDON

In the locker room getting ready for roll-call I'm tapped on the shoulder by the Sarge. Following him upstairs to the Ready-Room, there's a fit bird from Personnel sitting there along with my union rep and a higher-upper from the Yard. He reads a pre-prepared statement saying there's been a complaint made by a Mr and Mrs Hinselwood, alleging Assault and Battery. Goes on to say as of now, I'm suspended, with pay, pending further enquiries.
Suspended? With pay? Mr and Mrs Hinselwood? What the fuck? I don't know what to do, how will I face Janice? What about China, our takings? Fuck.

Andy.

THURSDAY 3rd JUNE 1982
1150 HOURS
AT HOME, NEW PARK AVENUE, EDMONTON

Janice is making us a cheese sandwich for lunch. She took the news of me being suspended surprisingly well actually, says it's part and parcel of being a copper. She knows it's for an alleged assault charge, while apprehending a pimp, but hasn't got a clue about Maisey, the fucking slag. I managed to grab China yesterday, just before leaving the Station, told him what's going on. He's solid, says he'll sort my takings as normal, that we got to look out for each other. The union rep says, in his experience, these types of things tend to blow over in a few weeks, with only their witness statement versus mine, worst case I'll get an advisory caution, but nothing official on my record, which is sweet. I love being a copper, just can't seem to stop being an idiot.

Andy.

THURSDAY 17th JUNE 1982
1505 HOURS
AT HOME, NEW PARK AVENUE, EDMONTON

Not written in a while. I'm like an injured puppy, all weak and feeble, somehow submitting to boring married life. I'm growing to hate Janice and the endless DIY jobs she's got me doing, just to keep busy, so she says. Got a call from John the other day, polite and official as usual, says he's heard about my suspension, but believes there's nothing in it, and, the witnesses will probably withdraw their statements once they see there's no profit to be made. Goes on to say Donnie is safe and sound and on his way home. Yeah, we won the war, Thatcher announced it a few days ago. Our lads have knocked shit out of them, sunk a few boats and downed a few planes, the argie-bargies are no match for us. Proud to be British.

Andy.

THURSDAY 5th JULY 1982
2030 HOURS
AT HOME, NEW PARK AVENUE, EDMONTON

Janice, the fat cow, has gone down the bingo with her equally fat, boring, ugly sister. Turns out we're off to Spain with her and her god-awful boring husband, Geoff, a fucking dull as dishwater light-ale drinking, golf handicap of 7 Bank Manager. Got an official letter today, inviting me to a disciplinary review meeting on Monday 19th July. About fucking time too. Gave my union rep Terry a call, says he's been informed of the incident and thinks it's a bloody disgrace that a stand-up guy like me has been suspended for so long, pay or no pay. Yeah, he's up for an argument, which is great. Bring it on.

Andy.

WEDNESDAY 21st JULY 1982
2344 HOURS
AT HOME, NEW PARK AVENUE, EDMONTON

Fucking twats. Hyde Park got bombed yesterday. The Household Cavalry do a morning walk-out through the Park, mainly for tourists I think, and the fucking Provo's let off a nail bomb, killing some men, horses too. Saw pictures of the mutilated animals on TV, turned my stomach, the fucking cowardly cunts. Horses, for fucks sake. The disciplinary lasted no more than twenty minutes. Terry was immense, took no shit and quickly got them to apologise for the aggro it's caused me, the sleepless nights and arguments with the missus. Little did he know, most of all that was actually true. While Maisey and Bev, or Mr and Mrs Hinselwood to give them their formal names, didn't actually withdraw their statements, with no corroboration to back any of it up, there's no case to answer. The panel suggested I take the rest of the week off on compassionate grounds, reporting fresh for duty next Monday. That's the minimum I deserve.

Andy.

MONDAY 26th JULY 1982
1215 HOURS
CHARING CROSS POLICE STATION, AGAR STREET, LONDON

First day back, it's all changed. China has been re-assigned to a specialist squad based in The Yard, and I'm back with Rich Tea. Yeah, a steadying influence, I get it. The higher-uppers don't really trust me 100%, they must have thought there was something in the Maisey and Bev thing. With China gone and Rich Tea back on the scene, fuck knows how I'll collect the takings, or whether China is still collecting. Off on holiday in a week or so, I'll have to sort all this out when I get back.

Andy.

SUNDAY 1st AUGUST 1982
2137 HOURS
AT HOME, NEW PARK AVENUE, EDMONTON

So, all packed, off on holiday tomorrow, early flight from Gatwick, Costa-del-boring-as-fuck here we come. Saving grace is we're meeting Mr and Mrs Boring at the hotel, meaning we don't have to travel with them. I won't be writing while I'm over there, can't risk Janice finding this little book and all its hidden secrets, nah, they'd be the fuse to a nuclear war. I'll go to Spain, soak up some sun, get her pissed as often as I can and knock the granny out of her while trying not to hang myself through boredom, or kill Geoff or June, the pair of ugly boring cunts. Ho-hum, we're all off to sunny Spain.

Adiós, Señor Andy!

TUESDAY 10th AUGUST 1982
1048 HOURS
CHARING CROSS POLICE STATION, AGAR STREET, LONDON

Spain is shit, too hot, too much olive oil, way too much garlic and fucking way-way-way too boring. No sex at all, hardly any drink, plus, we had to go on a couple of full-day excursions, one to Gibraltar, which to be fair was quite interesting, and one to a small village up in the mountains painted white with a fucking cemetery in what must have been the town square. Dear god, Geoff is a boring cunt, looks boring, talks boring plus, he hates football, says he's into Formula 1, for fucks sake. The only highlight was hearing him and June have it off in the room next door, with the headboard banging and her oohing and aahing, didn't think he had it in him, truth be told. Janice was disgusted, of course, even more because I found it funny. Still, gave me something to think about when I locked myself in the loo to knock one out. The indignity of me wanking into the fucking bath-tub, listening to dickhead Geoff reaching a climax while seeing Maisey sucking my cock in my mind's eye, how has it come to this. Janice and I argued a fair bit, most days we'd argue or just not speak, the boring fat-cow. Looking at her now, I don't know what I ever saw in her, even worse, I think she feels the same. If this is over, then it's over, but she can fuck off if she thinks I'll make it easy. She can fucking move out if she's that way minded, yeah, go live with Mr and Mrs Boring. Might see what Rich Tea thinks, he's been married a million years….

Andrew.

WEDNESDAY 11th AUGUST 1982
2330 HOURS
AT HOME, NEW PARK AVENUE, EDMONTON

Another argument with Janice tonight, this time about what to watch on TV, if you can believe that. Rich Tea says marriage is about compromise and understanding, about talking things through. Nah, what about excitement and sex and passion and feeling wanted? Sure, I feel bad knowing she's not happy, but I aint happy either. Better news on the China front though, he's been assigned to SO6, the Diplomatic Protection Squad, looking after foreign dignitaries when they arrive on special visits. Says it's mainly Middle-Eastern businessmen, who tend to be part of some royal family or other, says I should apply for a transfer, it's way more interesting than normal plod, and the overtime is plentiful. Says he can't do any more collections but, if I want to pick it up, he's fine with that, as long as he gets his fair share of the take. I'll ask Bee if he's up for it, he can be the heavy collecting debts while I'll stay in the shadows out of sight. Yeah, I thought about Will, but, other than running the West Ham firm, he's pretty straight nowadays, and Dex is busy with his legit car sales business. Bee's a big scary bastard who won't ask many questions, yeah, fits the bill perfectly.

Andy.

SUNDAY 29th AUGUST 1982
1810 HOURS
AT HOME, NEW PARK AVENUE, EDMONTON

Janice has gone round to her sisters, June, for a glass of wine, may or may not be back later. Fuck her and her shit Sunday dinners. I didn't go, but we lost yesterday, 2-one to Forrest. Saw the chaps later on though down the George at Silvertown, all pretty subdued. Pulling Bee to one side just as he's setting off for the carnival over at Ladbroke Grove, I tell him about my little bit of business, that the cunt shop-keepers are scared of their own shadows and are willing to pay whatever to make sure the police deal with any shit from punters. Of course he's up for a weekly trip into the West End, collecting best part of £300-quid and him pocketing a tonne, easy fucking money. Bingo, we're back in business.

Andy.

SUNDAY 31st OCTOBER 1982
2045 HOURS
AT HOME, NEW PARK AVENUE, EDMONTON

Total madness, Janice has gone, packed her bags and fucked off. Note left on the kitchen table saying she's not been happy in ages and knows I haven't been neither. She's off to stay at her mums, says some distance might help us think about the future. Think, about the future, fuck off, I don't need to think about shit, if she wants out, she can fuck off then, the fucking fat slag.

Andy.

MONDAY 3rd JANUARY 1983
1700 HOURS
CHARING CROSS POLICE STATION, AGAR STREET, LONDON

Months since I've written anything. New year though, new resolve, must get back on track. Janice has gone, for good, good for us both I think. Don't hold no grudges, just want her to be happy, want me to be happy too. Been knocking around the house all Christmas, other than Christmas day when I went back home and mum made Christmas lunch. Stayed till the day after boxing day, then took the old-fella and uncle Tommy down to West Ham, 3-one win against Swansea, nice. With all the chaps together, we had a right old laugh, no trouble though, hardly any away supporters actually. Just as well, didn't need those two old-men involved, nah, they've had their time. Thinking about uncle Tommy, I must go see Ken.

Andy.

FRIDAY 7th JANUARY 1983
2230 HOURS
AT HOME, NEW PARK AVENUE, EDMONTON

Saw Kenny today, fucking hell, I hate prison, especially the Scrubs. He looks okay, I suppose, put some weight on though. Says he's been taking a "philosophy" class, fuck knows why. He's still on about being set up, wanting revenge on the two pricks who grassed on him. I can't help him with any of that, told him to get his head down, serve his time and tough it out. Shrugging his shoulders, I see sadness in his eyes, regret even, a kind of melancholy, I think you'd call it. I'll try and see him more often, think he secretly looks forward to it, although he'll never admit it.

Andy.

MONDAY 17th JANUARY 1983
1935 HOURS
CHARING CROSS POLICE STATION, AGAR STREET, LONDON

The new year started with a bang, quite literally. At roll-call we're told about a record producer who got shot by an undercover SO19 officer in West London. Fuck knows what happened, but the officer fired three shots, so it seems it was no accident. Now, that's something that interests me, firearms, yeah, that's cool, bet they don't get much action though, just testing and practicing at the firing range. Anyhow, the higher-uppers have told us to be very conscious of public opinion, the press will be watching our every move now. I'll tell Bee to slow down with his cash collections this week, we don't need no aggravation.

Andy.

SUNDAY 6th FEBRUARY 1983
2315 HOURS
AT HOME, NEW PARK AVENUE, EDMONTON

Bored, bored, bored. Just back from a few pints down Canning Town, saw the boys there, well, Dex anyway. Says they had an away game at Birmingham yesterday, got done 3-nil, that's four we've lost on the bounce. Even worse, our boys got a hiding from the local crew, The Blue Noses. Dex reckons we held firm but a few of the lads got cut, and Will got himself arrested. Attending court tomorrow, he'll be bound over to keep the peace, I reckon. This place is pretty quiet, and fucking cold by the way, without Janice here. I really ought to get a bird or maybe even move, yeah, that's an idea. We bought this gaff 3-years ago so it's probably gone up in value. Fresh start and all that. I'll see what she thinks.

Andy.

THURSDAY 10th FEBRUARY 1983
1305 HOURS
CHARING CROSS POLICE STATION, AGAR STREET, LONDON

Rumour's rife about a serial killer being found in North London, yeah, a fucking serial killer. At last, something interesting. A plumber found some bones and skin, (yeah, that's disgusting), in the drains of some old house and called the police. The primary suspect seems to be a weirdo called "Andrews", who's already coughed for a couple of the killings, the sick cunt. Still, what a case to be involved with, much better than touring around the West End in a comfy old Rover.

Andy.

SATURDAY 12th FEBRUARY 1983
2236 HOURS
CHARING CROSS POLICE STATION, AGAR STREET, LONDON

Had a row with Janice about selling the house, (what a surprise), but, after no end of shouting, yelling and a fair number of insults, (on her part, the fat cow), she's agreed to sell. Got back-to-back days off next week so might think about where to live. Oh, and I've been bundled into our next home game against Brighton. Should be a giggle.

Andy.

MONDAY 14th FEBRUARY 1983
2200 HOURS
CHARING CROSS POLICE STATION, AGAR STREET, LONDON

I'm so fucking bored, feel restless. Still, this "Muswell-Hill Murderer", so the press are calling him, is at least a little bit interesting. Turns out, the fucking shirt-lifter's been chatting-up young boys, taking them back to his flat and ringing their necks before drowning them. Gossip in the Station is he dresses the dead bodies up and treats them like boyfriends, the sick piece of shit. Gays or not, they're someone's sons for fucks sake and don't deserve any of that. The press though, they're loving the seedy backstory and all the gory details, the fucking twats. They're the real villains here, whipping up hysteria and all that.

Andy.

SATURDAY 19th FEBRUARY 1983
2305 HOURS
MUM AND DADS, RUSCOE ROAD, CANNING TOWN

Just back from a quiet beer with the old-fella down the local, The Shakespeare's Arms, as I'm staying here tonight. Looking out my old bedroom window across the road to the Rodgers Road Estate where Will used to live, I'm taken back in time to when we were kids. It was a shit-hole back then too, six story blocks of maisonettes with net curtains and washing lines strung between buildings, it looks fucking grim. I'm almost grateful for my parents little semi, bless them, the "new houses" we used to call them. They've kept my room just like it was when I was a teenager, with the poster of the FA Cup winning team above my bed and my signed picture of Billy Bonds on the back of my door. Today was nice, went for a walk with me mum under the flyover towards the market, then past my old primary school. Told her all about Janice, that's it's properly over and probably a divorce, and that we're selling the house. She cried, and I'm sorry for that, but it felt like a weight's been lifted. Reckon I'll stay here for a bit while we sell up, it's for the best.

Jonesy.

SUNDAY 6th MARCH 1983
2205 HOURS
CHARING CROSS POLICE STATION, AGAR STREET, LONDON

Feel like shit, huge hangover. Met the chaps for a few bevvies, then down to London Bridge, yeah, completely the wrong direction, but, those Brighton fairies weren't gonna fuck themselves up, were they. Will arranged to meet them on the concourse outside the station for a straightener. We had 4 teams all travelling separately from different directions to avoid any police. My team were last to get there, but, soon as we arrive, right on que the Brighton crew steam in. To be fair, not many ran away so we end up scrapping for a few minutes before the bells and whistles came. Over the bridge into the City, me, Bee plus a few others catch a taxi to Upton Park where we all met up again. Fun times, plus, we won, 2-one, Goddard scoring, get in my son. Afterwards, we head to the Bunker Club for some drinks, then to the casino on Leicester Square. Before that though, me and Bee have some work to do, he's been having a problem with a shop on Manette Street, first trying to negotiate our fee down, then refusing to pay full stop. Slipping away from the chaps, we wander round. Outside, I slip on a balaclava while Bee has his mums tights on for fucks sake, now, that's funny. Steaming in, I chin the little fat fuck behind the counter while Bee rips the place a part and fingers the till. We get back maybe half an hour later with a couple of bags of dirty mags for the lads and £70 in cash. Good times!

Andy.

SATURDAY 19th MARCH 1983
1115 HOURS
MUM AND DADS, RUSCOE ROAD, CANNING TOWN

Away game today, so I'm here on my jacks. Just as well, Bee's not happy with me, nah. Turns out our friendly porno shop proprietor on Manette Street didn't appreciate us smashing the gaff up, so, when Bee goes round later in the week to pick up another collection, there's a team of Kung Fu Japs waiting for him, yelling all manner of hong-kong-chop-souey bullshit. A few short minutes later, Bee's outside on his arse surrounded by a load of nunchucka toting changs, nursing a bloody nose. Racing round here, he's ranting and raving, telling me a tonne a week isn't worth shit to him, so he's out. I'm bored of it too, to be honest, sure, I'll miss the money, but it's not a king's ransom, plus, if I ever get caught I'll lose my job and probably do some time. You don't want to be a copper in the nick. Fuck that.

Jonesy.

**TUESDAY 5th APRIL 1983
1015 HOURS
CHARING CROSS POLICE STATION, AGAR
STREET, LONDON**

At last, some proper action. The entire Station is buzzing. Huge armed robbery yesterday at a cash warehouse not far from here actually. Reports are sketchy, but, sounds like a well-armed team got into a warehouse dealing with cash delivery vans, having it away with a "significant" sum. The C.I.D. fellas are like pigs in shit, busying around, loving the drama. Us plod have been advised to increase visibility and ask around for anyone buying shit loads of expensive goods in the West End shops.

Andy.

WEDNESDAY 6th APRIL 1983
1130 HOURS
MUM AND DADS, RUSCOE ROAD, CANNING TOWN

Late shift today, got a bit of time to write some words. So, this big job was at a cash depot in Shoreditch, the chaps at the Station refer to it as "Fort Knox". It's a super secure warehouse dealing with cash collected from banks and shops, where it's counted and sorted then distributed back to the banks. Turns out, they broke in early morning and held the foreman and drivers hostage while they waited for the time-delay lock to trigger. Reports are they spoke with Irish accents, so, rumour is, they're IRA. Sounds an immense job, I'm so jealous of the team working the case.

Andy.

THURSDAY 7th APRIL 1983
2225 HOURS
CHARING CROSS POLICE STATION, AGAR STREET, LONDON

Still on the night shift, it's a real drag. Touring around the seedy back streets of London's West End has lost all its glamour, instead, everyone's talking about the big job in Shoreditch. Apparently, the robbers bound and gagged the drivers then poured petrol all over them, the poor fuckers must have been shitting themselves. Chit-chat in the canteen reckons they need the money for a bombing campaign over Christmas, and we'll all be seconded into new squads to deal with it, the West End being a prime target. Don't like the sound of that to be honest, don't want to be no cannon fodder for any Irish pricks, don't give a flying fuck about Ulster or any political bullshit.

Jonesy.

SATURDAY 9th APRIL 1983
0200 HOURS
CHARING CROSS POLICE STATION, AGAR STREET, LONDON

Day off tomorrow, then back on days, thank fuck. The Sarge grabs me earlier, saying a pal of his is running the recruitment for a new team of 150 officers attached to the special operations group dealing with organised crime, yeah, the robbery squad. I'm fucking totally interested, but don't want to apply if it's not 100% nailed on. Yeah, failed interviews count against you in the future, everyone knows that. Looks likely around 5-tonne of cash got taken from the Shoreditch job, yeah, it's measured in weight, not the sterling value. The main line of investigation is it's an inside job. the whole operation appears to be planned like a military operation with the gang knowing details of the drivers like the names of their children and even their pets, plus, although armed, not a single shot was fired, now, that's clever. With no shots, it's theft, carrying a maximum sentence 7-years, whereas, if shots were fired, then it's aggravated robbery with a maximum life sentence. Like I say, clever.

Andy.

TUESDAY 12th APRIL 1983
1120 HOURS
MUM AND DADS, RUSCOE ROAD, CANNING TOWN

Had a couple of pretty relaxing days off. West Ham won over the weekend, sweet, that's three on the bounce, we'll definitely finish mid table I reckon. Had a few jars with the old man last night down at the local, which was nice. Janice rang this morning, we've had an offer on the house. Not a bad price actually, would mean we could pay the mortgage off and each bank a couple of grand profit. Fuck it, I don't care about the money, just want out, want to close that particular chapter of my life. Sad though.

Andrew.

FRIDAY 22nd APRIL 1983
0910 HOURS
MUM AND DADS, RUSCOE ROAD, CANNING TOWN

Just told mum and dad I'll be leaving soon, need to get my own place, can't be in my twenties and still be living with my parents, plus, can't bring any new bird back here, can I. Been thinking about getting back out there, out on the pull, get me a new squeeze. Decent looking, (actually, more than decent I'd say), in good shape with a steady job, yeah, bit of a catch I reckon. More details are emerging about the Shoreditch job. Seems 1-tonne of cash equals £1m quid, so they got away with £5m, making it the biggest ever robbery in England, more than double the "great train robbery" in the 1960s. Been thinking more and more about this new robbery squad, the more I think about it, the more appealing it is. Can't see me driving around the West End with Rich Tea being a long-term career choice. Anyhow, I heard through a mate of a mate the Flying Squad are watching the Albion Pub in Stoke Newington, where Bee drinks now and again. Gave him a bell yesterday, from a telephone box just in case, telling him to ask no questions but steer clear of the gaff for a couple of weeks. Least I can do.

Andy.

SATURDAY 14th MAY 1983
2345 HOURS
MUM AND DADS, RUSCOE ROAD, CANNING TOWN

Been a while since I wrote, had lots of shit to sort out. Final game of the season today versus Coventry, at home, we won 4-two, Goddard got 2. No trouble at all, but still, had a right laugh with the chaps. Yesterday, the Sarge suggested again I apply for this new squad. I think it's a nod and a wink, not just him giving me some free advice. Got a new flat too, in Stepney, near Bethnal Green. The areas okay, I suppose, literally a 2-minute walk to the tube station, then 25 minutes to West End Central. Above an old suit making factory, it's a big gaff with two bedrooms and nice big windows, plus, a mate of Dex owns the entire block so the rent's next to nothing. Mum got a bit teary when I told her I was moving out, (again), but, like last time, she'll get over it.

Andy.

SATURDAY 21st MAY 1983
1150 HOURS
MY FLAT, GLOBE ROAD, STEPNEY

Moved in yesterday. Not got much by way of furniture yet, other than an old sofa from one of me mums friends, and a new bed I bought from a shop down near the tube station, plus Bee is dropping off a telly later today, hopefully. Went to see John yesterday, had a cup of tea with him, seemed really pleased to see me. We had a good chat for about an hour or so. He's been working on new procedures for dealing with suspects, new cautioning rules and questioning protocols, all coming out of the post-riot recommendations. Says he's heard the Shoreditch investigation is focusing on following the money trail, in particular, how it got moved across the city. Reckons they're trying to track down every white van for hire in London, a thankless task if you ask me. I tell him I'm thinking of moving on, maybe applying for the new robbery squad. Smiling, he says it's a great idea, reckons I should go for it. So, minds set, I'll apply.

Andy.

MONDAY 30th MAY 1983
0610 HOURS
CHARING CROSS POLICE STATION, AGAR STREET, LONDON

Interview tomorrow for the new SO71 squad, bit nervous, truth be told. Advice from the Sarge is to just be myself, but not too much, which is both funny and probably excellent advice too. Rich Tea, bless him, reckons I'll make a good investigator, says I can sniff a wrong-un. I like the old fella, his hearts in the right place even if his mind isn't. Roll on tomorrow.

Andy.

TUESDAY 31st MAY 1983
1135 HOURS
SO71 HEADQUARTERS, ISLINGTON POLICE STATION, TOLPUDDLE STREET, ISLINGTON

Just out of the interview, now in the shitter. I've taken to bringing this diary with me most places I go, I think it really does help. Anyhow, the interview went well. The panel included Terry Hughes, Chief Super, heading up the Command, David Fairbrother, DCI and, fuck me, me olemate Peter Smith, otherwise known as China. He's now DCI too, and, by all accounts, running the Shoreditch case. Their questions were pretty much standard interview fare, but they did ask, weirdly, how I might deal with being offered a bribe. Yeah, in the robbery squad, we're likely to rub shoulders with real wrong-uns and we'll be put under immense pressure by things like bribes. Responding textbook, I say I'd immediately document the event, then report it to seniors. Way too easy really.

Andy.

MONDAY 6th JUNE 1983
1830 HOURS
CHARING CROSS POLICE STATION, AGAR STREET, LONDON

Got a bit more information on the robbery squad. The new team will be based out of Islington apparently, an old Victorian yellow-brick building, quite imposing actually and surprisingly big, guess that's why they have the spare space for a large team like this. Bit surprised it's not based out of The Yard though, or perhaps Paddington. The building is currently being renovated, and, once finished, we'll have our own entrance just down the street, our own car park too. We also have access to an office at Walworth, doubt I'll visit though, I fucking hate the south-side. The team is 1 of 10 "commands" within the Serious and Organised Crime Directorate and is being beefed up due to the increasing sophistication and frequency of organised robberies, such as Shoreditch. Sounds ace, I love it.

Andy.

FRIDAY 10th JUNE 1983
1400 HOURS
CHARING CROSS POLICE STATION, AGAR STREET, LONDON

Fucking get in my son, nice one. Just been handed a letter by the Sarge, congratulating me on a successful interview, confirming my level-transfer to SO71, while I don't get any more pay, I'll get an unsociable hours allowance and a clothing allowance too as I'll pretty much be in civvies from now on. With Janice gone, new flat, new job, life's looking up, at last.

Happy Andy.

MONDAY 4th JULY 1983
1340 HOURS
SO71 HEADQUARTERS, ISLINGTON POLICE STATION, TOLPUDDLE STREET, ISLINGTON

What a morning, 11 of us started today and were given the background to the Command, our scope of service and how the squad will work, for example, we'll have direct access to Magistrates in case we need urgent warrants. We then had a talk to from Terry Hughes, Governor of the Command. A scouser, but what a guy. Mid 30's, gift of the gab, full of confidence bordering on arrogance, he's fucking excellent and can probably walk on water. Yeah, he knows he's good and wants the entire world to know he's the best at what he does. Walking among us, he's giving us both barrels about what he expects of his team and his high standards, all the while, he's staring deep into us all, winking at the right time then dropping down a pitch or two when it gets serious. The only issue I have is he has an annoying habit of finishing sentences with "la", "like" and "yah", it's already driving me mad. Breaking for lunch, we pop around the corner to a long street full of market stalls and shops, plonking ourselves in a greasy-spoon café called "Joe's" for a fry up. Fuck me, it's well tasty, better watch my waistline. Later this afternoon we'll learn more about our specific assignments.

Andy.

MONDAY 4th JULY 1983
2210 HOURS
MY FLAT, GLOBE ROAD, STEPNEY

What a first day, I'm exhausted, even more so because a few of us had a couple of pints after work at the local on the corner of Cloudsely Road, they have strippers there on a Friday lunchtime, apparently, nice one. Even better news, I've been assigned to the Shoreditch case. With China leading the team, I hope he knows I don't expect any special treatment, but, it's good we have a shared past. Says we have 3 areas of enquiry, following the cash, tracking suspects and researching the security firm. He hasn't decided which area I'll focus on, so for now, I'll do a bit on each to orientate through the team and familiarise myself with the case, which is fine by me, more I see the more I'll learn. It's going to be busy, but I can't wait.

Andy.

TUESDAY 19th JULY 1983
2350 HOURS
MY FLAT, GLOBE ROAD, STEPNEY

Been a couple of weeks since I last wrote, fuck me it's hectic. Along with the workload, which is huge, we have to fit in breakfasts, lunches, after work beers and field work too, it's taking its toll. I'll have to see Bee or Dex for some speed to keep me going. Fuck knows how the older chaps do it, maybe they're immune to it now or have built up a tolerance. Anyhow, the Shoreditch case is really cool. We now think it wasn't the IRA, but a London gang putting on Irish accents to put us off, a fucking smart idea. We have a few named individuals who might be involved, revolving around the landlord of Albion Pub in Stoke Newington, Clive Pett. We have a house across the road and have set up camp with a few long lens cameras. The main theory is, Pett is the planner, but wasn't actually involved in the robbery itself. Best we can hope for is "conspiracy" which is fuck all really. The team believe the guys responsible for the actual robbery have already fled to Spain, Costa Del Sol apparently, which is shit as we don't have an extradition treaty, something to do with them wanting Gibraltar back, well, they can fuck right off or get what the Argentinians got, the fish fucking fucks.

Andy.

THURSDAY 21st JULY 1983
1150 HOURS
SO71 HEADQUARTERS, ISLINGTON POLICE STATION, TOLPUDDLE STREET, ISLINGTON

Toilets here are miles better than the old stinking shitters back at Charring Cross, or, even worse, the decrepit cesspools in Brixton. Just having a quick shit before another fry up at Greasy Joes around the corner. China's been asking for volunteers to go to Spain, to investigate a local bank in small fishing village called La Cala de Mijas, and an apartment block in Marbella. The "cash team" believe the bank has received several huge deposits recently, and the apartment block has seen 7 apartments sold for cash in the last 2 months, yeah, it's got to be them. A week or so touring around Spain in the blazing summer sun, all expenses paid, yes please, I'll defo put my hand up.

Señor Andy.

FRIDAY 22nd JULY 1983
1450 HOURS
SO71 HEADQUARTERS, ISLINGTON POLICE STATION, TOLPUDDLE STREET, ISLINGTON

Fucking hell, feel a bit pissed to be honest. Just back from a few lunchtime beers with the lads, plus China. Had a good chat watching a couple of fat birds strip off to a Blondie soundtrack, then have a les-off between themselves, the fucking prick teasers. China is sound as a pound, says he did me a disservice way back, getting me involved in his protection business in Soho, especially me being a new recruit. Says he'll make sure he looks after me and there's no better place to build a career than here in Special Operations. Reckons the gaffer, Terry Hughes, is the most talented copper he's ever worked with and we're sure to learn loads from him. Anyhow, not so good news, I haven't been selected to go to Spain, nah, what's needed over there, apparently, is delicate diplomacy and a few wise old heads. I get it, makes sense, it's a smart decision. China says he knows he needs to get me more involved in front line field work, so is assigning me to watch one of the suspected ring-leaders, Fred Supps, who's been commuting to and from Spain pretty regularly for the past few months. The belief is he's ferrying cash over there bit by bit before he moves there permanently. From next week, I'll be on him, 3-days on, 4-days off. Exciting times.

Andy.

WEDNESDAY 27th JULY 1983
2315 HOURS
MY FLAT, GLOBE ROAD, STEPNEY

Exhausted. Covert field work is fucking hard work. You wouldn't think sitting on your arse watching wrong-uns is so tiring, but, fuck me, it is. Before I go to bed I have to write up my notes then hand them in tomorrow morning down at Walworth. Can't see the point really, I've just spent an hour briefing the relief team who've taken over from me, and I'll see them again in a few days' time when I take over their shift. Basically, this Supps chap, an old-school Kray Twins type gangster, owns a scrap yard right near Millwall Football Club, in between Bermondsey and New Cross, (I fucking hate Millwall). We have a room above a shop just down the road with a clear line of sight, been watching his every move, following him wherever he goes. If on foot, we'll chase down the back stairs and follow, if in his car, we'll radio to the car-team parked on the side road next to the shops, who'll do the honours. I've had one shift in the car and a few foot-follows, but, most of the time, I'm just watching and noting shit down, eating and sleeping where I can. The more experienced guys can fall asleep at a drop of a hat and drink cold soup straight from the can, the dirty dogs. As for Freddie Supps, he's a boring old cunt. A few trips to the betting shop and local café for a bacon butty, but nothing of any note. However, the other day he walked for about 20 mins to a shit-hole estate, just to use the pay phone. Suspicious, no doubt he's a wrong-un.

Andy.

MONDAY 1st AUGUST 1983
2315 HOURS
WATCH HOUSE, SURREY CANAL ROAD

It all went off today. Soon as I get there the relief team brief me and the others then disappear double-quick before I tidy the place up, (they're nothing short of disgusting pigs). Mid-morning, old Fred decides to go for a wander. Great. Out the door, down the stairs, I'm following 30 yards behind. Using my training, I wander along taking an interest in a few shop windows trying hard to blend in, (yeah right, a 6 foot 6, 16 stone stunner just blending in). Fred looks back toward me and our eyes meet, fuck. As he picks up the pace I know he's spotted me, shit, double-shit. I tail off, there's no point following, nah, he'll just give us the run around and take the piss. Told the on-duty Sarge, (a piece of shit lazy fuck called Hendricks), who, after a bollocking, tells me to note it all down in the logbook and think about my following technique, the cheeky fat fuck.

Andy.

FRIDAY 5th AUGUST 1983
1159 HOURS
MY FLAT, GLOBE ROAD, STEPNEY

What a few days. Still assign to old Fred, today topped it off. Following behind, I think he sees me, then as before, he picks up the pace to a slow jog, then, off the High Street, a sprint, if you can call it a sprint, he is 10-thousand years old after all. 5 minutes later, just before South Bermondsey train station, he slows and eventually stops. Bent over, hands on his knee's he's struggling for breath. Fuck me, he gasps looking up, you're a big-un, been on me a while, aint-cha. Listen, why'd you wanna-nick an old codger like me, for bugger-all as well. I shrug. Listen kiddo, how's about we help each other out, I'll look after you if you'll look after me, know what I mean. Looking along the approach road, I pull him into the little alleyway leading to the train station ticket office. Listen, I tell him, attempting to bribe an officer is an offense. Do me a favour, he smiles, you're all at it. Okay, if you're serious, we can maybe have a conversation, I say. Fuck knows where this came from, coppers instinct maybe. Smiling, he searches his pockets before handing me a fiver, then, a little blue bookies pen. Give us your number then soppy bollocks, he smiles. I scribble my home number, not sure why. Best time to call, he says, pocketing the note. I get off at nine, I say, so make it ten. Nod and a wink, he skulks away. Back at the watch-house, I call China and tell him what's happened. Pig-in-shit happy, he tells me I'm a fucking genius.

Well done Andy.

SATURDAY 6th AUGUST 1983
0115 HOURS
MY FLAT, GLOBE ROAD, STEPNEY

So, China's just called, I think from a pay-phone. He wanted to give me the low-down about what's really going on. Along with us staking out old Fred, another deep-cover covert team have been working with him to track the cash trail. This makes sense, explains how he's able to pop back and forth to Spain. Says for now, we'll have to play along with Fred, see where it takes us. Lowering his tone, says when Fred calls, I should be conscious of what's on and off tape, says there's likely to be a load of unaccounted for cash flying around, we might be able to pocket some if we're clever. Fucking hell, he's still in the game, the dirty bastard. Says Fred is old, reckless, thick as shit and taking it for granted we won't arrest him, that we're only really after the guys that planned it all and not a bit-part player like him. Mate, got lots to think about. Still not sure I can trust China, in fact, this might be an elaborate test or something.

Andy.

SATURDAY 6th AUGUST 1983
2340 HOURS
MY FLAT, GLOBE ROAD, STEPNEY

Telecoms team got here at 1800-hours, ready to set everything up. Unplugging my normal phone, they want me to use a dual receiver tape machine thing, plus a huge carry case full of wires which, they tell me, along with a similar machine at the telephone exchange, can trace where the call is coming from. 2200-hours on the dot, Fred calls. Alright young-un, listen, he says. You up for a trip to Spain fetching a few bags through customs, I'll make it worth your while, see you right. Right-right, I nod along, all the while looking to China for ques. Tickets booked from Gatwick on the red-eye Friday night, what you reckon kiddo, Freddie asks. Explaining I don't have that level of clout, I tell him if he really wants to do it, I can rope in my buddy who has air-side clearance, (i.e. China), but we'll both need 10 large. You robbing toe-rag, he laughs. I'll sort you 5 for the intro, and your buddy 10, how's about that. What a fool, he doesn't ask who my "buddy" is, also, disclosing an actual amount implicates him to bribery, clearly he's an idiot, desperate too. Phone down, China says we'll follow his trail through Spain, then, when the right's time, nick him for his part in the robbery plus bribery of an officer. I won't be doing any bag carrying though, too dangerous apparently, but, surprise-surprise, what do you know, China will do it personally. Sounds fishy. Either way, I don't give a shit, just being in on all this is enough for me. Yeah, my time will come.

Andy.

SUNDAY 4th SEPTEMBER 1983
1100 HOURS
MY FLAT, GLOBE ROAD, STEPNEY

Hectic busy the last few weeks. Old Fred's in custody now, the fucking old fool. China did indeed carry some bags through customs, with best part of 80-grand inside. He stayed with Fred for a few days in a tasty villa in that fishing village, the one all the South London villains seem to gravitate to. Popping out in the middle of the night, he gets a message to Interpol in Lyon who liaise with the Spanish police and arrange for Fred to get sent back to blighty, fuck the fact we don't have an extradition agreement. Picking him up in the dead of night, they drive straight to the RAF base at Gibraltar and a waiting military plane. No trial, no appeals, nothing, just straight on the plane and fuck off back to England. Me and China got called out at roll-call as having done a "superb job-yah", (as Terry says), tells us we've been nominated for some type of commendation. Sweet, makes a change from a bollocking. Later in the week, I have a pint with China who hands me an envelope with 5 grand in, saying it's my part of the "take". Fuck knows whether this is what Fred paid him or whether he skimmed a bit from the suitcases, but, I'll ask no questions. Says he and Hughes are impressed with my work, says the higher-uppers feel the same way too. Double Sweet.

Andy.

SATURDAY 1st OCTOBER 1983
1047 HOURS
MY FLAT, GLOBE ROAD, STEPNEY

Out on the lash last night, end up at a pub on the Isle of Dogs, the Ferry House I think it was, before going on to a shit-hole of a club in Shadwell. Pulled a bit of a looker, she's just left actually. Walking her to the tube station, I stop off at the corner shop to get some paracetamol, fuck me, my head's pounding. She's not bad looking, reckon I'll give her a call in the week see if she wants to meet up again. Stoke away today, Bee and the others have gone up there on the train to have it large. We should beat them no problem, we've won 6 of the first 7 games of the season. While out last night, I bump into that Millwall geezer, The Greek, who I met a while back at the Bunker Club. Interestingly, he's there to meet Dex, they had a bit of business to attend to, which is weird, Dex has never said he works with any Millwall. More drinks chaps, Dex smiles, heading to the bar before The Greek leans over. Oi, listen, he whispers, you did us all a favour sorting out old Freddie Supps, a fucking liability. Nodding, without showing any sign of recognition, I don't want any talk about the job. Dex comes back with 3-pints and I see The Greek chuck him a wink. As well as telling him I'm a copper, Dex has obviously told him about the Shoreditch job. Fuck me, I need to be careful what I tell him.

Andy.

THURSDAY 13th OCTOBER 1983
1150 HOURS
GREASY JOE'S CAFE, CHAPEL MARKET, ISLINGTON

The last few weeks have been boring. The Shoreditch job is winding down now a few of the ringleaders have been arrested, the others are known to us but on the run. Apparently £2m of the take has already been recovered, no doubt after some grubby DCI has taken their share too. I've been reassigned to a team looking at a gang of balaclava wearing sawn-off shotgun wrong-uns, partial to robbing post offices. Mainly paperwork, classifying historic cases, looking for similarities, boring behind the desk shite. Liverpool away at the weekend, the entire crew are heading up there, apart from me, I have to work. Still, got a night out planned with Claire instead, the bird I met the night I bumped into The Greek. Seen her a few times since, just for dinner, then for a drinks. She seems to want to take things slow, which is weird because we've already fucked. Still, greasy fry-up's on its way. Get in.

Handy Andy.

SUNDAY 16th OCTOBER 1983
1440 HOURS
MY FLAT, GLOBE ROAD, STEPNEY

So, here we are again. Had a blinding night last night, with Claire. She lives Walthamstow way, knows Dex's younger sister apparently, yeah, they both went to the same hairdressing school. We had a drink in the Blind Beggar, just up the road in Bethnal Green, then popped over the road for a curry, then, back here for some how's-your-father. Let's just say, she can fuck. Not as depraved as Maisey, but 100-times better than Janice, the boring fat cow, who'll just lay there moaning for a minute or two before I dump my load. Nah, Claire's active, appreciative and energetic, knows what she wants. I think I like her. Only downside is that she sort of knows Dex, not sure how close she is with his sister, but I don't need her sharing any bedroom talk. He's been on my mind a lot recently. Terry Hughes was busying around the office during the week, asking if anyone had anything on a "hooligan car dealer", based in Woodford, no doubt referring to him. Head down, I watch carefully to see if anybody in the office pipes up, but, nobody does, which is good. With that, plus The Greek saying him and Dex were doing "some business", I'm feeling un-fucking-easy all of a sudden. Fuck Dex.

Andy.

WEDNESDAY 26th OCTOBER
1830 HOURS
SO71 HEADQUARTERS, ISLINGTON POLICE STATION, TOLPUDDLE STREET, ISLINGTON

Not written for a while, just taking a shit before heading home. Had a few more dates with Claire and been busy with work looking at 2 cases now, the south London post office gang and helping with some loose ends on the Shoreditch case, paper trailing the money into the City where some dodgy fuck legal firm seems to have been buying up a string of betting shops across London, with their revenue suddenly and magically being boosted overnight by around 200%. China says it's a classic money laundering technique, fucked if I know, I'll just collect the evidence then hand it over to the solicitors and higher-uppers. Going to see Kenny next week, I'll ask him what he thinks, him being an old-school city-boy. Oh, best news ever, we beat Bury 10-nil last night, yes 10, fucking get in my son. 4 for golden boy Goddard too.

Andy.

THURSDAY 3rd NOVEMBER 1983
1915 HOURS
MY FLAT, GLOBE ROAD, STEPNEY

Just waiting for Claire to pop round for some supper, (as she calls it, I call it any excuse for a good seeing too). I really like her you know, not sure it'll go anywhere though, we'll see. Went to see Kenny yesterday, still putting on weight the fat cunt, he's talking about being moved to a lower category prison, out near Norwich. Means I won't be able to visit him as regular, which, to be honest, suits me fine. Mentioning the betting shop laundering scam, laughing, he says most City firms, including the big banks, love cash businesses. Apparently, they charge more fees for cash transactions, partly to cover genuine handling costs and partly because they know most of it's dirty money needing to be cleaned. I'll feed this back to Terry Hughes, might earn me some brownie-points.

Andy.

FRIDAY 4th NOVEMBER 1983
2030 HOURS
MY FLAT, GLOBE ROAD, STEPNEY

Excellent news, just seen on the telly the weirdo who killed all those gay boys in Muswell Hill has been sentenced, life with a minimum of 25. Good, should have been longer, should have been the death sentence actually. He'll be sent to Broadmoor, no doubt, where hopefully one of the insane inmates will slit his throat or bum him to death. Disgusting.

Andy.

TUESDAY 8th NOVEMBER 1983
0630 HOURS
SO71 HEADQUARTERS, ISLINGTON POLICE STATION, TOLPUDDLE STREET, ISLINGTON

Shift starts at 0700-hours, so taking a quick shit, might actually knock one out come to think about it. Been seeing Claire pretty much every other night recently, we're taking it in turns round at each other's gaff. She shares a house in Walthamstow with another fit bird call Nikki, (with 2 K's). At work, we have a "rogues gallery" up in the main office now with the faces of "people of interest", the idea being if anyone gets a whisper about any of them, to inform the copper working their case. The other day I see a face I recognise, yeah, The Greek. Did some research on the quiet, seems his real name is Mehmet Ahmet, born 1961 in Güzelyali, Turkey, moved to London in '66. Records suggest he's pretty high up in the Millwall firm, working with a serious villain called "Harry the Dog". Apart from hooliganism, he's suspected of dealing wholesale resin as well as being involved in various armed robberies. Good to know for when I broach the subject with Dex, yeah, I got to know what he has or hasn't told him about me. We've got Wolves on Saturday, at home. I'm currently down on the rota to work, but I'm hoping I can swap it so I can go.

Andy.

SATURDAY 12th NOVEMBER 1983
1005 HOURS
MY FLAT, GLOBE ROAD, STEPNEY

Walked Claire round to the tube, she's working today, says she's saving for a deposit on her own shop so is working all hours. Reckons with her take and the rent from maybe 2 other chairs, she'll treble what she takes home now, even after costs. Who'd have thought hairdressing could be so profitable. Meeting the chaps later at the George on Silvertown Way, from there, we'll get a few taxis to the ground. Can't wait to be honest, haven't seen the chaps in while, will be nice to catch up.

Andy.

SUNDAY 13th NOVEMBER 1983
1150 HOURS
SO71 HEADQUARTERS, ISLINGTON POLICE STATION, TOLPUDDLE STREET, ISLINGTON

Thought about calling in sick today, but, fuck it, can't keep on doing that, nah, I'll just plough through. Sunday is usually quiet, most guys are writing up case work or just counting the hours till we're done. Banging headache, way too many beers with the lads last night. 3-nil win, Goddard, (surely a few goals away from an England call-up), and Booker, (the old-fella), both scoring. Had an almighty row before kick-off, yeah, it was ace. The traffic was carnage, so we get dropped off on Boundary Road, maybe a 15-minute walk to the Boleyn. Passing the flats on the left, with the tall tower-block behind, we see maybe a couple dozen Wolves giving it large, so, naturally, me and the chaps plus a few faces we know give chase through the estate onto Haigh Road. Gets to the park down there, fuck me, there's 100's of the Wolves grouped together, shouting and goading with that "Bollock Head" fella right in the middle. Spinning around, there's about 40 of us, all up for it. Will's shouting "nobody runs, nobody hides" as we steam in, having it large, before chasing out of there double quick. I got a whack across the head, Dex a lovely black eye while Bee walks away unscathed, having smashed his way through about 10 of them. I should probably give a statement down the local nick, I might have been seen.

Andy.

SUNDAY 13th NOVEMBER 1983
1750 HOURS
SO71 HEADQUARTERS, ISLINGTON POLICE STATION, TOLPUDDLE STREET, ISLINGTON

Just clocked off. Saw China earlier, had a decent chat. Reckons I shouldn't bother giving a statement, I was off-duty plus, in any case, sounds like handbags anyway. Handbags, fuck off, I personally saw a fair amount of blood and a few fellas laid out cold. I'll follow his lead though, he knows what he's doing. He's been assigned to a new case, following a group of heavy hitters who've previously been suspects on a few cash van robberies. Serious villains, rumour is they're planning something "big", but, as yet, no target's been identified. China says if it kicks off, he'll request I'm assigned to the case. Sweet, sounds right up my street.

Andy.

FRIDAY 18th NOVEMBER 1983
1830 HOURS
MY FLAT, GLOBE ROAD, STEPNEY

Dex has just left. Waiting outside when I got back from work, says he was passing so thought he'd pop in. Stepney is miles from his place, nah, he's after a quiet word. His shiner has turned purple now, suits him actually, gives him character, better than his skinny-as-a-rake-gelled-back-dark-hair-Hitler-moustache look. After some small-talk, he goes on about Will being too big for his boots, wondered whether it's time he stepped down as leader of the crew. Woah, that's big talk. He's on a roll though, says Bee is getting worse too, he'll end up getting us all nicked. What do you really want, Dex, I ask. Alright darling, he smiles, keep your knickers on. Goes on to say he's been flogging a few dodgy motors recently, some with fake MOT certificates, others without logbooks. I tell him these are relatively low-level crimes, if they ever got to court, he'll probably take a fine or suspended sentence. Says he's been knocking out a bit of cannabis resin too, just to mates of mates mainly. No bother, I tell him, that's low level shit. Says, actually, he's been punting pretty large quantities, a pound at a time, a grand a spin. Ah, that's different, that's serious shit. I tell him he must be careful but hold back from telling him they were asking about him by name down the Station, nah, that'd freak him out. Joining the dots though, I get this is how he and The Greek know each other, and why Hughes was asking about him.

Clever-clever Andy.

SATURDAY 19th NOVEMBER 1983
0615 HOURS
MY FLAT, GLOBE ROAD, STEPNEY

Quick one, leaving for work in a second, morning glory, just had a brilliant blow-job from Claire, fucking hell, felt like my arsehole was pumping out of my balls. 23-years old, that's the first time I've finished that way. She's ace.

Andy.

MONDAY 21st NOVEMBER 1983
1015 HOURS
SO71 HEADQUARTERS, ISLINGTON POLICE STATION, TOLPUDDLE STREET, ISLINGTON

Just attended an all-staff meeting, the entire SO71 directorate were crammed into the canteen. A hush descends as Terry Hughes walks in, fuck me, he's so cool. Ohh-kay-ladies, he smiles, welcome to my dancefloor where we'll trip the light fandango to the beat of my drum, you understand, of course you do. Cool. So, my lickle-cherubs, listen the fuck up-yah. With a Scouse accent he sounds cool as fuck. Some of you may be aware we've been tracking significant activity associated with a bunch of toe-rags from South East London. The way he stresses each syllable is so powerful. As yet-yah, we don't know the exact details, but, as sure as shit flows from my arsehole, they're planning something big, big ben big, ding-fucking-dong big, know what I mean-yah. We all chuckle. He goes on to say for the next 2 weeks, we're all officially "on-call" meaning we can be called-in within 20 minutes notice. China says we'll receive an on-call allowance of £15 per day plus any overtime we do at double-time. Great, a meaty case plus extra cash, things are looking up.

Andy.

MONDAY 21st NOVEMBER 1983
2325 HOURS
MY FLAT, GLOBE ROAD, STEPNEY

Got a taxi back, on China's account, just as well as the meter read £17. Downed a fair few beers to be honest, feeling a bit pissed now, tiered too. He invited me out earlier for a "private chat", but, for my own protection and sanity come to think of it, I know I have to write this down. Just me and him for the first hour, later joined by the lads, he fills me in on what Hughes was talking about at the all-staff meeting, "Operation Eagle" he calls it. Says they've been watching a few of firms for 12 months or so, one of which did the Shoreditch robbery, the other 2 remain active, with intent. One are from South East London, the other from Queens Park, West London. He goes on to say we have a number of potential targets identified, a few bank cash transit depots, such as Shoreditch, some large banks and the main post office sorting office in Farringdon. Although details are sketchy, he reckons plans are definitely being made. Rumour is something big will happen any day now, so, he wants me on the team, and this is a bit of a recruitment session I reckon. At last, some proper adventure.

Andy.

TUESDAY 22nd NOVEMBER 1983
1845 HOURS
WALWORTH POLICE STATION, MANNOR LANE, WALWORTH

Down at this shit-hole today, an old Victoria nick, stinking of piss, surrounded by sink-estates and gutter snipes. This is where "Eagle" operates from. China has just done a briefing, basically replaying what he told me yesterday down the pub. The new team look okay too, I recognise a few faces yeah, a couple of guys who were on the rotation at the Freddie Supps watch-house in Bermondsey, plus an older guy called Fairbrother, who I met on the first day at SO71. The whole team feels tense and on edge, there's a definite air of anticipation, I love it.

Andy.

WEDNESDAY 23rd NOVEMBER 1983
2205 HOURS
HESTON SERVICES, M4 MOTORWAY, WESTBOUND.

Needed a shit, any excuse to get away from mister-boring-as-fuck, aka Fairbrother. We're following, well, trying to follow a couple of fellas in a tasty little Golf, (we're in the Renault 25 piece of shit pool car). Two white fellas, mid-thirties, been all around the houses of South West London, now heading west on the M4. Not sure about this, feels like a waste of time, they have the look of plumbers or brickies, certainly not armed robbers. They're currently having a cup of tea, look to be waiting for someone maybe. Can't be long, got to go.

Andy.

THURSDAY 24th NOVEMBER 1983
0737 HOURS
WALWORTH POLICE STATION, MANNOR LANE, WALWORTH

Fuck me, under-cover work is exhausting. Managed to get a few hours sleep on Tuesday night, but, since then, we've been on the case 24/7. Driving through the night last night following those two numpty's, we end up in Maidenhead. Technically, it's Thames Valley territory, but the Met, accordingly to Fairbrother, has an agreement to extend across without prior authority if on an active operation. While looking like average Joes, these two guys are most certainly suspect. Who the fuck drives around London for hours, then across the M4 to Maidenhead, only to park up outside a shit-tip terraced house. We watch for a few hours while Fairbrother calls it in and local C.I.D take over "watch" duties. Sitting there watching paint dry, he tells me all about his garden and what grass feed he uses, his allotment too, which he tends at the weekends or whenever he had a day off. Mate, he must only be in his 30s but seems like he's in his 60's. No way I want to turn into that, the boring fuck.

Andy.

THURSDAY 24th NOVEMBER 1983
1610 HOURS
MY FLAT, GLOBE ROAD, STEPNEY

Debriefed China and "Red Command" back at base, they're collating all the information coming in. We now have around 40 officers deployed on "watch jobs", which is a big deployment by any standard. For now, I've been sent home for a few hours kip, got to be back down at Walworth for 0600-hours tomorrow. Might give Claire a call, see what she's up to.

Andy.

FRIDAY 25th NOVEMBER 1983
2100 HOURS
WALWORTH POLICE STATION, MANNOR LANE, WALWORTH

Long day today, got here as planned at 0600, (0543 to be precise). Lots of SO71 here as well as officers from SO7, the mother fucking Flying Squad. Something big is definitely going down. Been told we're on a "through-er" tonight, nobody can go home. The Watch Teams are out, busying away all around London, so I'm due to go into Red Command, reviewing the inbound intel and deciding what's worthy of follow-up, and what's crap. Red Command is located on the top floor, with multiple radio receivers and a huge map with flags showing the approximate location each "Watch Team". On another wall, a rogues gallery of suspects, with notes scribbled underneath. There's a load of admin and secretaries in there too, including a few fit birds to be honest, all typing up notes when officers pass them formal "WR" record slips. It's all go, I love it.

Andy.

SATURDAY 26th NOVEMBER 1983
0530 HOURS
WALWORTH POLICE STATION, MANNOR LANE, WALWORTH

Fuck me, been on it all night, drunk way too much coffee, feel like crap now. Been receiving tonnes of information from the Watch Teams, informants too, it's pandemonium if I'm honest. We've also received details of all robberies undertaken over the past week. From what we can gather, there's no real pattern or "Modus Operandi", (as Hughes calls it). Can you believe yesterday we had 4 armed robberies in London. 2 post offices, 1 bank, (a failed attempt), and a postman held up at gun-point, no doubt the fucks were looking for giro-cheques. It's a fucking war-zone out there.

Andy.

SATURDAY 26th NOVEMBER 1983
1005 HOURS
WALWORTH POLICE STATION, MANNOR LANE, WALWORTH

Received sketchy reports from local plod at around 0815-hours about an armed robbery at a warehouse near Heathrow Airport. China and a load of SO7 Flying Squad chased out of here pronto, to be fair, I've never seen him move so quick. Reports are the 8 guys working there were held up, bound, gagged and dowsed in petrol, exactly how the Shoreditch crew operated. Fuck.

Andy.

SATURDAY 26th NOVEMBER 1983
1425 HOURS
WALWORTH POLICE STATION, MANNOR LANE, WALWORTH

China's just got back, along with Hughes, they're busy debriefing each Watch Team individually, mate, they had faces like thunder. More info on the armed gang, they're thought to be at least 6 strong and have taken approximately £2m in cash, plus precious metals and diamonds. I'm still collating info, trying to account for all for the whereabouts of each of our suspects. I'm told every second counts, with every passing moment the cash gets further away and harder to track.

Andy.

SATURDAY 26th NOVEMBER 1983
1745 HOURS
WALWORTH POLICE STATION, MANNOR LANE, WALWORTH

A professional job, fuck me, way more planned than Shoreditch. The warehouse, like many around the Airport, didn't have much by way of physical security, other than a "Swiss Safe" needing 2 keys and 2 codes, each in the possession of two specific employees. That they managed to get in suggests an inside job to me. All the employees with access to keys and codes have been arrested, currently being held at different nicks across London. The press are everywhere, TV too. China is livid, turns out 3 of the Watch Teams had lost their markers in the few hours before the blag, including Fairbrother, (the boring cunt), who lost his suspect at around 0430, but didn't call it in till gone 0600, rumour is the cunt fell asleep. He's sure to get at least a bollocking, thank fuck I wasn't posted with him. I'm exhausted to be honest, hope to be sent home soon.

Andy.

SUNDAY 27th NOVEMBER 1983
1100 HOURS
MY FLAT, GLOBE ROAD, STEPNEY

Got back late last night, went straight to bed, due back in at Midday. Watching the news, they reckon it's £3m cash, plus up to 3 tonne of gold. 3 fucking tonne? Reports say the warehouse was a "bonded facility" used by middle-eastern royalty as they move cash, gold and other valuable assets around the world. I'll learn more later.

Andy.

SUNDAY 27th NOVEMBER 1983
1600 HOURS
WALWORTH POLICE STATION, MANNOR LANE, WALWORTH

It's been confirmed, £3m cash plus 3-tonne or £25m in gold. Fucking hell, that's way bigger than Shoreditch. A primary suspect has been identified, Richard Campbell, a low-ish level villain from Peckham, not far from here actually. Serving 18 months years back for aggravated assault, he's been implicated on a few cash van robberies over the years but nothing ever really stuck. A couple of separate snouts have given us his name, so he's well worth looking into. Closer to home, (too close for my liking), he's one of the suspects me and Fairbrother tracked to Maidenhead during that all-nigher. Fuck me, who could tell.

Andy.

TUESDAY 29th NOVEMBER 1983
1600 HOURS
WALWORTH POLICE STATION, MANNOR LANE, WALWORTH

Working my bollocks off on the case, it's backbreaking, boring work to be honest. We have 4 separate teams, one on the suspects, one on the victims, who all remain suspects, (I'm on this team), one on the "take", and one looking at wider support the villains might have had, cars, equipment and all that. Terry Hughes says it's 100%, dead-cert, cock-on-the-block an inside job-yah. Mate, he cracks me up with the way he speaks, he knows his shit though. Missed the football this weekend, we drew 1-one with Man U, shit game by all accounts. I'll be on this case for a while I reckon, likely to miss a fair few games.

Andy.

SATURDAY 3rd DECEMBER 1983
1130 HOURS
MY FLAT, GLOBE ROAD, STEPNEY

First proper day off in a few weeks, thank god. I'll see Claire later, maybe a meal or the pictures perhaps, I don't know, but defo a serious session later on, yeah, I reckon we could go steady. The Heathrow Job is all over the news, the press fucking love it. We've connected one of the guards, Tony Green to Richard Campell, the main suspect, through a friend of a friend. It's pretty tentative at the moment but China is close to challenging him with this during questioning. The "take" team have had good news, the cash is all UK Sterling, meaning the numbered notes will be easier to track. The gold bars have serial numbers on too, which, according to Hughes, will mean they'll probably need to be smelted down before being pushed into circulation. Can't wait to see Claire later.

Andy.

MONDAY, 5th DECEMBER 1983
0940 HOURS
WALWORTH POLICE STATION, MANNOR LANE, WALWORTH

Hate working down here in this shithole, takes fucking ages to get here too. However, I'm in a good mood all things considered, yeah, had a blinding weekend. Claire is an absolute loon, the other night we end up at the Bunker Club in the West End and she somehow gets hold of some cocaine. Serious shit, a bit like speed, makes you feel 10-feet tall and, I got to say, fucking on it is something else. Turns out she likes a line or two at the weekend, but didn't want to say anything with me being Old Bill. Fuck it, I'm off duty, I can do what I want. Seeing her again tomorrow night round at hers, can't wait. Back on the Heathrow job, the other guards turn out to be clean, at least, no history of criminality and their families haven't changed their behaviour patterns since the robbery. All eyes are now focused on this fuck-wit Tony Green, what an arsehole.

Andy.

WEDNESDAY, 7th DECEMBER 1983
1315 HOURS
GREASY JOE'S CAFE, CHAPEL MARKET, ISLINGTON

Back up to SO71 HQ, an all-hands briefing by Terry Hughes. He tends to do these monthly, or when anything juicy is going on. Listen, he says as a quiet shush spreads across the canteen. Thank you all for your hard work-yah, it's unheard of to have two huge blags so close together. Fuck me, he's not wrong. Our work on the Shoreditch job, he continues, is all but complete, with the case passing over to the wigs and the briefs to bring to trial and deal with all the politics and tabloids. Yeah, spot on, some minor b-movie Hollywood actor ponce seems to be vaguely involved in the money laundering, so, of course, the Press are all over that. From here on in-yah, our attention will move to the Heathrow job, in fucking particular, the money trail. I love this guy, even though he's a scouser, he's quality. Mark my words my pedigree chums, he says, over my cold-grey dead body are these pig-dogs getting away with it-yah. Yeah, he's super cool, he knows it, I know it, fuck me, everyone knows it.

Andy.

THURSDAY, 8th DECEMBER 1983
2055 HOURS
CAT AND CRADLE PUB, CLOUDESLEY ROAD, ISLINGTON

China invited me for a beer with him after work, so, here I am four pints in and a bit pissed. He's just popped to the shitter, says he's expecting to execute some arrests in the next week so needs guys he can trust, wants me boots on the ground with him. Excellent, all this paperwork I've been dealing with is bollocks. Also, tells me Fairbrother is on a disciplinary for allowing his marker to give him the run around. Interesting. I reckon he's told me because I was with Fairbrother when we tailed the same guy, he wants to know what I know, whether Fairbrother is a wrong-un. Straight down the line, I haven't got a clue. Hope to fuck he doesn't think I'm in any way involved.

Andy.

SATURDAY, 10th DECEMBER 1983
0710 HOURS
WALWORTH POLICE STATION, MANNOR LANE, WALWORTH

This is more like it, in at 0600-hours for a briefing with China plus a few others. Today we're supporting the "take" team, 3 units tracking a single suspect, me and China being one of the units. We're meeting up at a warehouse in Stratford, East London. Perfect, my neck of the woods.

Andy.

SUNDAY, 11th DECEMBER 1983
1440 HOURS
WALWORTH POLICE STATION, MANNOR LANE, WALWORTH

Fucking hell, another through-er, right through the night, hopefully get to go home soon. So, we chased up to Stratford yesterday, waited a few hours outside the industrial unit before following a beautiful 1977 Rolls Royce, in gold. Yeah, a fucking Roller, can you believe it, a gold one too, that's just taking the piss, rubbing our noses in it. Took some great photos of the suspect plus two other guys loading a large, heavy looking wooden create into the boot. They must have known we were following because they circled around and double-backed a few times, before a leisurely jaunt out to Southend of Sea. China says the main suspect is Barry Robbins, a well-known "fence" who seems to have made a massive leap from dealing in stollen cars to armed robbery of gold bullion. Anyhow, he has fish and chips on the sea-front, then a couple of pints in the Borough Hotel overlooking the pier, before setting back off to London. Appearing to head back to the warehouse in Stratford, he drives right by before heading through the Blackwall tunnel into South-East London. We journey through Greenwich on the A2, then into Kent, all the while we're keeping our distance. Eventually he pulls into an expensive looking mansion in the village of Coxheath. We watch for a few hours before handing over to local C.I.D. As much as I like Southend, mate, following suspects is exhausting. I'm fucked.

Andy.

SATURDAY, 17th DECEMBER 1983
1000 HOURS
MY FLAT, GLOBE ROAD, STEPNEY

What a week. The lads are off to Nottingham today, an important fixture, Forrest have been on a bit of a run, plus, Will reckons the Nottingham firm are looking to have our pants down, so he's assembled a pretty tasty crew of about 200. I've agreed with him and the others I can't really do away games no more, gutted. Dex came round during the week saying his "mate", who owns this gaff, is looking to raise the rent. I'm beginning to think it's actually Dex who owns this place, but, to avoid any complications, he's letting on it's a mate. Even so, at £20 a week, it's still a steal and, more importantly, I sort of think of it as home now. Back to the Heathrow job, last Thursday we, well, Terry Hughes, never one to miss out of a decent publicity stunt, formally arrests both Tony Green, the "inside man" and also the chap we followed, Barry Robbins, who managed to leave 3-grand of Heathrow cash in the boot of his Rolls, the stupid half-a-brain-cell idiot fuck-wit.

Andy.

SUNDAY, 18th DECEMBER 1983
0944 HOURS
CLAIRES HOUSE, EXMOUTH ROAD, WALTHAMSTOW

Just got up, what a sight. The winter sun cracking through the tree right outside her window beams on to her pretty face. It's sappy, but I watch her sleep for a while before she smiles, dreaming of me, hopefully. Gently kissing her cheek, she tilts her head and our mouths meet. We fucked, but not like before, this was slow and passionate, the orgasm lasting for ages. Yeah, I get it, I sound like a girl but seriously, I can feel myself growing to like her more and more, I think she feels the same. She's asked if I'll go with her down to Dagenham Docks, meet her old man. He's in a nursing home or something, lost his marbles hasn't he. The closer we get to Christmas, the more she talks about family, I think she misses her mum, her dad too. So, last night, trying to avoid the chaps who were due back into London at 2100-hours, we stay local and had a nice Chinese and a few beers before coming back here to watch a video and snort some coke, yeah, she loves coke. Anyhow, walking out of the restaurant, we only bump into The Greek and his missuses, (a tasty Cypriot bird with curly black hair, big round eyes and even bigger tits), plus her mum, dad and younger brother and sister. Turns out her family live down the road in Leyton and they're out for a family meal. All nice and cordial, we exchange a few words before The Greek suggests we meet up for a proper beer, talk business and all that. "Business and all that", nah, don't think so mate.

Andy.

WEDNESDAY, 21st DECEMBER 1983
2110 HOURS
MY FLAT, GLOBE ROAD, STEPNEY

The Heathrow job is full on, lots of irons in the fire, lots of different shouts to follow up and all that. Barry Robbins, the suspect we arrested, has been really helpful with our enquiries, spilling the beans all over the place. He's given us the name of a guy called Bobby Love, (I know, a great name), reckons he's responsible for smelting the gold. Says he's a small time gold dealer with years-old receipts for bullion, which he uses to move the dodgy gold around. Yeah, I can hear the defence, "no sir, this isn't the Heathrow gold, this is my own gold, I've had it for years and, I have a receipt to prove it too," that sort of thing. He's also mentioned, under caution, he's aware of a few coppers on the take, fuck me, what a bombshell. While he didn't mention him by name, we all know he must be talking about Fairbrother, (or maybe China to be fair). Hard to believe, a quiet, family guy career-copper is a snitch, he wouldn't say boo to a goose to be honest. Fuck me.

Andy.

TUESDAY, 27th DECEMBER 1983
2220 HOURS
CLAIRES HOUSE, EXMOUTH ROAD, WALTHAMSTOW

Been here since Christmas Eve, haven't had time to write any shit down. It's been nice, being here, with her, just the two of us yeah, her flat mate Nikki has gone to stay with her folks up North. Christmas Day, she says she loves me, but looks to regret it straight away, flushing up and all that, but, you know what, the feelings mutual, and I told her the same. Heathrow update, all eyes are on this prick from Kent, Bobby Love, who's suspected to be the one shifting the gold. We have 3 teams watching him, each in rotation, but, the sneaky fuck, his Manor House mansion thing has deep woodland surrounding the perimeter, making long-lens observation difficult. We'll get him though, no doubt about it. The cash seems to be in circulation now, with the odd note here and there being found by the Bank clearing houses. This is good news, once the villains start spending, it's easier to spot them. Southampton away today, we're on a bad run, lost the last two. Also, more bad news, Bee got arrested in Nottingham, currently on remand for affray. Could be pretty serious, depending on what the judge is like, hooliganism is being taken more seriously nowadays.

Andy.

FRIDAY, 6th JANUARY 1984
1005 HOURS
SO71 HEADQUARTERS, ISLINGTON POLICE STATION, TOLPUDDLE STREET, ISLINGTON

Just had what I think was a bollocking, but might have been a word to the wise, I don't know. Terry Hughes has a series of meetings with most of us in China's team, says the Heathrow job has uncovered a fair amount of corruption, with coppers on the take, some actually colluding with the crim's, like Fairbrother, (who, by the way, has been arrested and is subject to an "Anonymity Order"). Hughes says, in his scouse accent, SO71 is clean-yah, that he's personally reviewed every single member of staff's background and is as sure as his uncle-peter's-a-paedophile, the unit is clean. However, says he's acutely aware of my background and previous disciplinary issues, and has made it clear he'll not tolerate any sexual relations with Toms, no matter how sexy they are, and definitely no football shenanigans, (his words), especially with a shite team like West Ham, (again, his words, cheeky bastard). Says I should get my head down and go steady with that "bit of skirt" in Walthamstow and make something of my career. I think it was positive, in the end.

Andy.

TUESDAY, 3rd APRIL 1984
1230 HOURS
SO71 HEADQUARTERS, ISLINGTON POLICE STATION, TOLPUDDLE STREET, ISLINGTON

Just realised I haven't written anything for months, probably the longest time ever. Me and Claire are sound, not living together, yet, although she's talking about it more and more. Work is okay too, I'm currently cultivating a few snouts as well as working on the Heathrow job, although it's mostly loose ends now, we pretty much know who did it, caught some of them while most of the others have fled to Costa-del-Crime. Bee gets out on Friday. He's done nearly 5 months in total, kept his head down and done his time. Can't believe it's been 5 months to be honest. It'll be good to see him and the lads again, it's been ages since we all got together.

Andy.

SATURDAY, 7th APRIL 1984
0811 HOURS
MY FLAT, GLOBE ROAD, STEPNEY

Got the shits, bad. Went out last night, Bee's welcome home party, down the George, on Silvertown Way. Must have been a bad pint or that shitty speed we were dabbing. Had a good chat with Dex, says The Greek wants to get me, as Old Bill, on his payroll, keep him out of trouble. He can fuck right off if he thinks that's me, I aint for sale, especially not to him, the prick. Working later, then seeing Claire tomorrow.

Andy.

WEDNESDAY, 18th APRIL 1984
0720 HOURS
SO71 HEADQUARTERS, ISLINGTON POLICE STATION, TOLPUDDLE STREET, ISLINGTON

Just been briefed about a female officer being shot yesterday outside an Embassy in central London. Fucking hell. Based at Bow Street, she's deployed in uniform to monitor a protest outside the gaff when some fucking idiot starts letting off shots, and she gets hit. The fucking fools have locked themselves inside, claiming diplomatic immunity or some other bollocks. China reckons we're now on "high" alert so villains might choose to take advantage of the situation and try it on. We must be careful.

Andy.

FRIDAY, 20th APRIL 1984
1440 HOURS
SO71 HEADQUARTERS, ISLINGTON POLICE
STATION, TOLPUDDLE STREET, ISLINGTON

Just about to head over the road to the Cat and Cradle pub, meeting some of the lads there, including China. Met with John earlier for a cup of tea at New Scotland Yard. Got to say, he looks hot to trot, proper desk-bound politician now. Asking him about my career and how to get on, he reckons going for the Sarge exams would be great, and, he for one would recommend me if that would help. Work wise, he's leading a review of the Met at the moment, looking for "operational efficiencies" and a better structure to support increased local policing. I'm sort of proud of him you know, only a few years ago we were at Hendon together with him talking like a fairy with a plum up his arse, yet now, he's this high-powered higher-upper. He goes on to say with UK foreign policy causing unrest in the middle-east, even more resources are being deployed into covert counter-intelligence type work. Honestly, his head must be bursting spinning all these plates. Anyhow, off for beer and strippers now. Nice.

Andy.

FRIDAY, 27th APRIL 1984
1940 HOURS
MY FLAT, GLOBE ROAD, STEPNEY

The worlds going to shit, utter shit. The siege at the Embassy is still going on. Yeah, over the past few days, we've had the fucking military bomb disposal teams chasing all over London and we've been providing cover. These fucking arabic-types have been planting bombs everywhere, in support of the pricks who shot and killed our colleague. Get the snipers out then send in the fucking SAS, I say. Thankfully, for us in SO71, it's been pretty quiet, the fears of dickheads trying it on has subsided a bit, plus the Heathrow job is pretty much wound down now. China is off too, apparently, says he can't tell me what his next job is, other than it's a promotion, and deemed "top secret". For now, I'll be reporting direct to Hughes. Got the weekend off, heading up to Claires in a bit.

Andy.

TUESDAY, 15th MAY 1984
0650 HOURS
SO71 HEADQUARTERS, ISLINGTON POLICE STATION, TOLPUDDLE STREET, ISLINGTON

One win in the last 10 games, not good enough, it's wank, thank fuck the season's over. We finished mid-table, just missing out on Europe, but, we all agree, the manager has to go, he's taken us as far as he can. Been mad busy at home, Claire's moved in with me in Stepney, plus I'm due to take the Sarge exams in a few weeks. Yeah, it's all go.

Andy.

THURSDAY, 17th MAY 1984
1350 HOURS
GREASY JOE'S CAFE, CHAPEL MARKET, ISLINGTON

Had a long lunch with John, he's here on an official visit meeting with Chief Super Hughes. We end up sharing breakfast, me a full English, egg on toast for him. With him sitting there sharp suited in full uniform, I look a pleb in my under-cover civvies. Looks the part though, he's now "Commander", something like four grades from Commissioner. Says Hughes is well respected by the higher-uppers and will do well, even though his manner is a "tad crude", (his words, not mine). Anyhow, he's given me some good advice about the exams, and the interview after where I'll be put under pressure to see how I'll react. He's also given me a Criminal Law book, huge bastard of a book, and, bless him, he's highlighted a few chapters for me to read. What a great guy.

Andy.

THURSDAY, 31st MAY 1984
1030 HOURS
SO71 HEADQUARTERS, ISLINGTON POLICE STATION, TOLPUDDLE STREET, ISLINGTON

Sarge exam tomorrow, shitting myself actually. Been reading no end of books as well as doing previous exam papers as practice. Apparently, there are 6 sections, Law, Crime, Evidence, Procedure, Traffic and General Policing. By all accounts, this particular exam is going to be one tough bastard. A new evidence-based procedure called "PACE" is being implemented later this year so everyone's shitting themselves. After the exam there's an interview where performance in current role and any recommendations or commendations are reviewed. It's up at Hendon, 1000-hours, been told to expect to be there till 1600-hours. Will need a stiff drink afterwards, for sure.

Andy.

FRIDAY, 1st JUNE 1984
2015 HOURS
MY FLAT, GLOBE ROAD, STEPNEY

Knacked, fucking hell, that was hard. I haven't written as much since school, even the initial entry exam to get into Hendon wasn't as tough. Fuck knows how I've done, might have fucked it up, probably have. Claire will be home any minute, maybe we can celebrate with a delicious blow-job.

Andy.

SATURDAY, 2nd JUNE 1984
2355 HOURS
MY FLAT, GLOBE ROAD, STEPNEY

Just back from an "afternoon" with the boys. What started as a few quiet ones down at Bethnal Green, turned into a magical mystery tour across London. Just after midday me and Dex are having a lovely quiet one, chatting about work and all that when Will walks in, already half-pissed. He sees a few of the Arsenal crew over the other side of the saloon, so, (naturally), launches a pint glass their way. Spills out to the High Road and, after a quick scuffle, they scarper, so we kick the living shit out of Mister Unlucky who gets left behind. Will, the mug, stuffs a business card in his coat pocket, something about "meeting the Inter City Boys", the fucking idiot, sounds like a '70's prog-rock band. For some peace and quiet, I take them to the Cat and Cradle, up near work, and have a good couple of hours playing pool. We go for a curry and Bee joins us saying he has it on good authority "Harry-the-Dog", the legendary leader of Millwall's top team is on a night out with the wife at a back-street shithole nightclub called "Bonnies" in Sydenham. Fuck me, what a scalp if we can get him. Couple of taxi's flagged down, we head South. Full of slags, there's no sign of any Millwall hooligans, only a few young plebs, so we have a few drinks and head back to London Bridge for a kebab under the railway arches. Fucking waste of time, thank you Bee!

Andy.

THURSDAY, 8th JUNE 1984
1440 HOURS
SO71 HEADQUARTERS, ISLINGTON POLICE
STATION, TOLPUDDLE STREET, ISLINGTON

Terry Hughes follows me into the toilet early this morning. I take a seat for my morning constitutional, while I hear him at the urinal. Talking over the stall, after some, morning-how-you-doing chit-chat, he asks me if I might be interested in a posting to a new squad, COG10, a new unit within the Crime Operations Group specifically focused on "intelligence-based policing". To be fair, it sounds decent, although, intelligence, me? Says it's a brand-new unit to be officially launched later in the year, reckons I should think about it-lad, talk it through with the missus, see what she thinks. Food for thought. Can't stop thinking about Will and his business cards though, what the fuck is he on? The new season is weeks away, yet he's already beginning to piss me off.

Andy.

FRIDAY, 15th JUNE 1984
1205 HOURS
SO71 HEADQUARTERS, ISLINGTON POLICE STATION, TOLPUDDLE STREET, ISLINGTON

Just seen a memo asking for volunteers to do 2 weeks up north in Yorkshire, helping with the Miners' strike, the poor buggers. Says it includes double-time for the entire 2 weeks, plus a guaranteed 20-hours overtime as well as bed, breakfast and transport too. Sounds a good deal to be fair, a few of the chaps in the locker room sound like they're up for it. I'm not though, fuck that, apart from it not being my scene, back in uniform and all that, I'm actually with the dirty Northerners. These mines still have coal in them yet Maggie is hell bent on smashing the unions and is playing hard-ball. Might be my working-class background or my Dad's morals he's drilled into me, I don't know. Keep politics out of this bullshit!

Andy.

SUNDAY, 17th JUNE 1984
1434 HOURS
MY FLAT, GLOBE ROAD, STEPNEY

Fucking shock of my life, Terry Hughes has just been round here, un-announced. Me and Claire just had a roast chicken dinner, (top notch by the way), and were considering a bit of Sunday afternoon how's-your-father when he knocks. All serious, he sits down opposite us both. Glad you're both in-yah, he nods. Got a proposition for-yah kiddo. Claire tightens her grip on my hand. A fella with your talent is wasted pissing-in-the-wind with robberies and thefts, you and I both know that-yah. I nod, he's not wrong, I'm dogs bollocks good. Okay, he smiles, this is the deal. Sign up for COG10, working with me, deep undercover-yah, way deep, deeper than the deep-blue-sea, you see? Claires grip gets tighter. See, intelligence lead Policing is the future, we've been playing catch up with the crims for yonks now-lad, what we need to do is covertly observe, watch and even influence the villains-yah, rather than waiting for gutter-snipe-snakes to cough, feeding us dog-shit info, er-hum, excuse my language-lah. He's right, I get it, it's what John talked about ages ago way back at Hendon. Sounds interesting, I say. Listen-lad, you need some time-yah, talk it through with your good-lady, he winks at Claire. Gotta-say-lad, you're-batting there-aren't-yah-kiddo. Cheeky bastard. But, listen big-lad, I like you, you got to know, once you're in, you're in deep my friend, no going back deep, yah-understand? Yeah, I think I do.

Andy.

TUESDAY, 19th JUNE 1984
1734 HOURS
SO71 HEADQUARTERS, ISLINGTON POLICE STATION, TOLPUDDLE STREET, ISLINGTON

Just called into Hughes' office. Ah, big-lad, he smiles. Thought about my proposition, my little petal? Even when he's patronising, he's still super cool. Okay-course you have, now, listen-yah, you need to know this is hush-hush, you'll have to sign the Official Secrets Act and all that-palavah. You'll be given a letter, signed by the Commissioner and the Home Secretary, explaining your job, making sure you're not carted off to the nick. Andy, no joke, this is deadly serious shit-yah, you understand what I'm saying-lad. That letter, that lump of solid gold is your official get out of jail card-yah, your get-me-out-of-everything card, it'll make very clear you have been, currently are and continue to be a serving officer. Why do I need that, I ask. Good question Bamber-fucking-Gascoigne, so listen-up. To go deep, you'll need a fucking copper-bottomed back-story, so, you'll be dishonourably discharged-yah, marched out of here with a boot up your shiny red-raw arse. You'll go on massive bender and fall back in with your happy-hammers mates. You'll be one of them, live like them, fuck like them, snort like them, eat, drink and shit like them-yah, all the while, my beauty, feeding nuggets of pure gold back to us. Fuck me, this sounds both shit-scary scary and totally fucking excellent at the same time. Word to the wise-doh, he leans back in his chair. Go have a chat with bum-boy-Cummings, then, let's talk again-yah. I get up and leave, sort of shell-shocked, if I'm honest. If he's for real, this is indeed serious shit, I'll do well to seek Johns council.

Andy.

WEDNESDAY, 20th JUNE 1984
0645 HOURS
MY FLAT, GLOBE ROAD, STEPNEY

About to leave for work, she's blow-drying her hair while I munch Shredded Wheat. She doesn't want me to accept Hughes' offer, says under-cover work is way too dodgy. I haven't even told her about the discharge bit yet, she'll properly shit herself with that. What a conundrum. Oh yeah, I've passed my Sargant's exams, and, if I join COG10, Hughes will bump me to Inspector. 2-promotions, can't quite believe it all to be honest.

Andy.

FRIDAY, 22nd JUNE 1984
1650 HOURS
SO71 HEADQUARTERS, ISLINGTON POLICE STATION, TOLPUDDLE STREET, ISLINGTON

Saw John today, he knows all about Hughes, his offer and the new COG10 squad, says he helped design it's "terms of reference" and "statutory safeguards", whatever the fuck that means. Goes on to say this level of covert work has never been attempted before, by any Force, anywhere in the world, but, with the growing sophistication of the global criminal fraternity, (his words, not mine), we need to take drastic action. They'll be about 2-dozen live operatives, plus hierarchical and administrative support. Says the initial deployment is for 6 months, with a formal review at that point. Says I'll have to check-in at a specific nick once every 2-weeks to provide a statement in the presence of at least a Chief Superintendent. Says all Laws must be observed and obeyed, and I must immediately report any serious offences, Crown Court type stuff like grievous bodily harm, firearms, rape and other sexual offences, also murder, attempted murder or conspiracy to murder. The most serious I've ever seen him, says he couldn't think of anyone better than me to do this though. Can't wait now, sounds the dogs.

Andy.

TUESDAY, 26th JUNE 1984
1122 HOURS
SO71 HEADQUARTERS, ISLINGTON POLICE
STATION, TOLPUDDLE STREET, ISLINGTON

Doubts, so many doubts, so much to think about, so much I don't know. Do I be brave and go for it, or, sit on my hands and crack on. How often will an opportunity like this come up though, to be involved in something so trail-blazing. Yeah, maybe I'll do it for 6 months, take the double promotion then come back as an Inspector, that'd work, that sounds like a plan.

Andy.

WEDNESDAY, 27th JUNE 1984
1025 HOURS
SO71 HEADQUARTERS, ISLINGTON POLICE STATION, TOLPUDDLE STREET, ISLINGTON

I'm in. Just told Hughes, he's like a pig in shit. Says I'll need to spend a few days getting ready, speaking with a psychologist, an ethics lawyer and a chap called Drucker-Smith, Commander of the Crime Operations Group, in effect, Hughes' boss. He'll then arrange for an "incident" to occur, whereby I'll be suspended for 6 weeks or thereabouts, before being summarily dismissed. He'll be my personal handler and I must only ever contact him while in the field, or via a Chief Superintendent if at a nick. Under no circumstances am I to mention Hughes, COG10 or anyone else concerned to anyone, either civilian, or police. Can't say I'm not nervous, but, excited all at the same time.

Andy.

FRIDAY, 29th JUNE 1984
2125 HOURS
MY FLAT, GLOBE ROAD, STEPNEY

Glad the weeks over, speaking no end of shite to no end of fucking idiots. The psychologist delved into all sorts, my mum, my dad, uncle Tommy, Kenny too. Talking about relationships, she has a file on me an inch big and knows about Janice, Claire too, the nosey cow, I nearly fucking cried at one point. The lawyer guy, oh god, dull as dishwater, quoting all types of laws, processes and blah-blah-blah bullshit, I've already forgotten everything he said. Most interesting was the chat with Nigel Drucker-Smith, or, "please call me Nige", mister nice-guy. Telling me it's a very brave thing I'm doing, that he's in awe of "chaps like me" and, 30-years younger, he'd be "at the front of the line" for such an assignment. What a load of crap. Anyway, I'm in.

Andy.

SUNDAY, 1st JULY 1984
1147 HOURS
MY FLAT, GLOBE ROAD, STEPNEY

Guess where I've been? The cells at Bethnal Green, just got back, spent the night there. I've been charged with Actual Bodily Harm under the Offences against the Person Act, maximum sentence is 5-years. I can't believe it, this is for real, this aint no Terry Hughes plan, it's all gone to bollocks. I'm having a quiet night out with Claire, few beers and a curry, it's all good. She's rubbing my cock under the table and I'm getting into a pretty good rhythm. Outside, I flag a taxi down, it's only a 15-minute walk home but I can't wait to get her knickers off when this cocksucker jogs over with his two mates and opens the taxi door. Sorry mate, I say, this one's mine. Be a good lad, catch the next one eh, he smiles. Catch the next one? Be a good fucking lad? Fuck off. Quick one-two-three combo and he's rolling on the floor holding his face while his mates are yelling, backing away scared. A passing patrol car spins around and stops, then I get arrested. For fucks sake.

Andy.

MONDAY, 2nd JULY 1984
0750 HOURS
SO71 HEADQUARTERS, ISLINGTON POLICE STATION, TOLPUDDLE STREET, ISLINGTON

Been here for an hour already. Soon as I got in, I'm ordered to hand over my warrant card and to wait outside Hughes' office, all the while fellow coppers, colleagues and friends walk by giving me a wide birth, staring down their judgemental noses at me. I'll be suspended now and any move to COG10 will be out of the window. Bollocks.

Fuck wit Jones.

MONDAY, 2nd JULY 1984
1035 HOURS
MY FLAT, GLOBE ROAD, STEPNEY

Great news, in fact, brilliant news. I'm now officially suspended, with pay, yes, WITH pay!!! Into Hughes' office, he's smiling, beaming ear to ear. Well, fuck me-lad, he says. What are you like, eh? Err, what, I say. Done us a right-old favour-yah, no need for me to concoct no cock-and-bull-bullshit about you having light fingers. Sorry, what? This is it-lad, this is your exit-yah, you're gone now. Oh, right, I smile. You'll be suspended from now, give it a month or so and you'll be up on a charge. You'll lose your shit at the hearing, properly am-dram it up-lad, then you'll be dismissed. In the meantime, you'll get your letter-yah, then you'll begin to build your crim-persona with those West Ham fuck-wits, shouldn't be too difficult for a man with your talents, right-kid? Right, I sigh, thought I was a goner. Far from it-lah, he smiles. Al-doh, you got to watch that chicken-vindaloo-fiery temper, that'll get you fucked up the arse-yah. We then do some shouting and screaming for effect, while both pissing ourselves laughing before I go clear my locker. No doubt I'll be the talk of the Station for a week or so, just what my cover story needs.

Andy.

TUESDAY, 3rd JULY 1984
0815 HOURS
MY FLAT, GLOBE ROAD, STEPNEY

Wanted a lay-in today, maybe some early morning inny-outy, but no, we're up at 0630-hours, arguing. She isn't happy with the suspension, I'm surprised by her reaction truth be told. Fuck me, I haven't told her about the dismissal part, nah, that's a security risk at the very least. As far as she's concerned, I'm a very sexy hot head who's been suspended, and fucked my chances of promotion. If I'm honest, I'm in a right dilemma about whether to tell her or not. If I do, she'll be okay with it, I think, but it might place her at risk. If I don't tell her, then I'm just a stupid dickhead and a failed copper, she won't want that.

Andy.

SATURDAY, 7th JULY 1984
1200 HOURS
MY FLAT, GLOBE ROAD, STEPNEY

So, she's gone. Massive rows all week long, she just can't cope with me not being a copper no more, she's almost embarrassed I've been suspended, seems all her dreams rested on me being a "steady-eddie". Can't believe it to be fair, I'm so into her, still am, but, true-colours, that's what they say. It's only through hard times you really see what people are made of. Gutted actually, properly gutted.

Andy.

SUNDAY, 8th JULY 1984
1530 HOURS
MY FLAT, GLOBE ROAD, STEPNEY

Lord god, what a hangover. Got a call yesterday from Dex, says he's heard about me being suspended and about what happened with Claire. He invites me round to his for a beer, no problem, it's only a couple of stops on the tube. After a few beers we get a taxi to Hollywood's in Romford, full of cheeky-chappy Essex boys and wanna-be-gangster types, the fucking idiots. The whole crew are down there too including Will and Bee, with Bee holding court as he does nowadays, yeah, since his release, he's almost like a celebrity. Will, on the other hand, is drifting into a murky underworld, associating with fellas who run the doors at some clubs in Southend and along the Essex coast. Beers, spliffs and cocaine later, we're having a right-old knees up, with loads of totty dancing around too. I end up getting tossed off upstairs on the balcony overlooking the dancefloor. Just what I needed actually, although the tight cow didn't want a proper fucking, or even to give me her number. Reckon she might have been a Tom, Dex must have bunged her a few quid to sort me out. From there, a 40-minute taxi ride back to Will's for a piss-up. Fuck me, his bird was vexed, giving him 100-tonnes of grief. He cornered me, for an age, telling me about the forthcoming season, that he wants to ramp up the crew, leave everyone in no mistake the ICB are the top team in England. Rolled back here at 0815-hours this morning. Back in with the lads already, good work fella.

Andy.

TUESDAY, 10th JULY 1984
1330 HOURS
MY FLAT, GLOBE ROAD, STEPNEY

Bored, bored, bored. I thought having all this time on my hands would be relaxing, a doddle, a piece of piss but fuck me, I'm so bored already, it's only been a week. Might have a wank.

Bored Andy, the most bored guy in the world…

TUESDAY, 17th JULY 1984
0915 HOURS
MY FLAT, GLOBE ROAD, STEPNEY

Up early, out for a run, should at least keep myself fit. Got back to find a letter on the doormat, inviting me to a disciplinary review on Friday 10th August, says I can invite a union rep to accompany me, and the review will be chaired by Terry Hughes, Chief Superintendent of Special Operations Unit 71. This is it.

Andy.

MONDAY, 23rd JULY 1984
0810 HOURS
MY FLAT, GLOBE ROAD, STEPNEY

Off to meet Paulson later, the union guy, he'll brief me on what to expect, what to say, what not to say, blah-blah-blah. Poor bugger's grafted hard on my case, all in vain though as we already know the outcome. Will called me yesterday, maybe the day before, can't remember now, asking if I wanted to come "on tour". Him, Bee and a few of the hardcore are off to a pre-season tour of northern Europe. Says we'll have a few laughs, a few beers, maybe test out the European crews before heading to Amsterdam for a dirty weekend. You know what, I'm up for it, up for it big time, but, I've got this hearing right bang in the middle of it. When I tell him, he's affronted, hurt almost, saying Dex has cried off too, demanding I at least attend the pre-season games here in England, the first one in a weeks time, at some poxy non-league club near Reading. Yeah, I'm up for that, no fucking problem my end buddy.

Andy.

**WEDNESDAY, 1st AUGUST 1984
1230 HOURS
MY FLAT, GLOBE ROAD, STEPNEY**

Getting ready for the away game, meeting the lads down the George at Silvertown, from there, into central London then a train to Reading. No idea about the crew we're due to meet, can't imagine they'll be any match for us though. As for the game, I'm keen to see our new centre-back signed from Fulham, got high hopes. After the disappointment of last season, we need more than a few better players.

Andy.

THURSDAY, 2nd AUGUST 1984
0945 HOURS
NEW SCOTLAND YARD, ST JAMES' PARK, WESTMINSTER

Game last night was bit of a disappointment, we won, but let 3 in, so much for our new centre-back! Even though Golden Boy Goddard wasn't playing we still scored 4, which is encouraging. As for the home crew, fucking mugs, ran off as soon as they saw us, we were only 100-up too. Early morning start heading down here. Fucking hate this place, full of higher-uppers who haven't got a clue about real policing, still, at least the shitters here are way nicer than every single Station I've ever been in. Half expected to see John here, but nah, he's not about, instead, I have a briefing with Drucker-Smith about my new role.

Andy.

THURSDAY, 2nd AUGUST 1984
1134 HOURS
BENCH OVERLOOKING THE THAMES AND COUNTY HALL, WESTMINSTER BRIDGE

Finished my session with Drucker-Smith, shit, he's dull, gives me some pearls of wisdom about deep undercover assignments and covert policing in general, reminding me there's a fine line between protecting my backstory and committing offenses. He suggests I make notes every day, recording any issues or events that might at a later stage be used against me, or the Met. If in any doubt, he says, go to any nick to make a voluntary official statement. I tell him about this very book, that I've been keeping a diary, (of sorts), ever since Hendon. An excellent idea, he recommends I should keep on making entries for my own sanity if nothing else. Bless him, says if ever it gets too much, or I want out to contact him directly. He goes on to tell me other than Hughes and himself, officially the "Authorising Officer", nobody else knows specifically about me, or the other COG10 officers. He says there's a COG10 Steering Committee of several senior officers who'll review every individual deployment weekly to ensure probity and standards. All massively formal, but, makes me feel pretty secure actually. I didn't mention John to him, that's for me, my secret back-door, my exit route in case any of this goes to shit. Oh yeah, he also gave me a letter, I'll have a gander…

Andy.

THURSDAY, 2nd AUGUST 1984
1215 HOURS
BENCH OVERLOOKING THE THAMES AND COUNTY HALL, WESTMINSTER BRIDGE

"OFFICIAL MARKING - TOP SECERET.

To Whom It May Concern,

Officer Andrew David Jones, Police Identification number UX838, Pay Number 256734 is officially deployed by her Majesty's Metropolitan Police within the Crime Operations Group, reporting directly to Commander Drucker-Smith.

By virtue of this letter, Officer Jones has continuously been and continues to be a serving Police Officer within the Metropolitan Police, deployed into a Specialist Unit with the security classification of "TOP SECRET". Upon presentation of this letter, Officer Jones shall be granted every courtesy and treated with the utmost discretion.

It's signed by Sir David Armstrong, Commissioner of the Metropolitan Police and Rt Hon Leo Clementine, Home Secretary on behalf of Her Majesty's Government. Below each signature is an embossed seal. Drucker-Smith suggests I keep this letter safe, maybe a safe deposit box, with multiple copies held safely at different locations such as my parents' house. Not quite a get out of jail card, but pretty damn close.

Andy.

FRIDAY, 10th AUGUST 1984
1220 HOURS
SO71 HEADQUARTERS, ISLINGTON POLICE STATION, TOLPUDDLE STREET, ISLINGTON

That's it, I'm officially dismissed from the Met. Ordinarily, my hearing would have been at New Scotland Yard, but Hughes thought it would have a bigger impact if done here. I had a session with Hughes first thing, where he gave me my initial briefing for the COG10 job, working the Heathrow job, (of all the possible jobs), trying to gather info on the guy we suspect is the leader, Richard Campbell. The last few guys working the case reckon he used to date an old girlfriend of a Millwall hooligan called Mehmet Ahmet, otherwise known as, yep, you guessed it, "The Greek". They also mention he's a known associate of my old school buddy, Dexter Bissell, aka, "Dex". Fuck me, makes complete sense why I've been put forward for this. A few of the guys, including China, have suggested a "leaving drink" at the Cat and Cradle over lunch.

Andy.

WEDNESDAY, 15th AUGUST 1984
1010 HOURS
MY FLAT, GLOBE ROAD, STEPNEY

Not a lot brings me to tears, but that did. Can you believe I got a letter from Rich Tea, dear old Derek from West End Central. Says he's heard about me being discharged and wanted to wish me luck, reckons I'm a good kid, says, even if policing isn't for me, he hopes I'll find contentment in life. Bless him. I hadn't really thought about how all this must look to other folk, obviously Claire was pissed, but what about my parents. They know I'm up on a disciplinary, but they'll be crushed when they hear this, I can't tell them the truth. Then there's Janice, this'll prove she made the right decision to do one and leave. It's hard to believe I'm still a copper, yet, can't tell a single soul the truth.

Andy.

SATURDAY, 18th AUGUST 1984
1240 HOURS
MY FLAT, GLOBE ROAD, STEPNEY

Found a gym not far from here, down near Aldgate tube, a proper place with weights and a boxing ring, heavy bags too. Been down a few times over the past week or so, decent guys down there, they know their onions. Got to keep fit, keep sharp, way too easy to sit on my arse wanking myself into oblivion. Gave Hughes a call yesterday just to check in, he's sound "yah", still sounds like a scouse twat though. Tells me to begin asking around, try to get some info on Campbell, fuck knows how, it's not as easy as he thinks. Oh, bit of gossip, he tells me China's in the shit. Apparently, he's running a surveillance job and was listening in to some Saudi diplomats phone conversations, but the suspect was having work done on his phone-line and an engineer traced it back. The suspect has raised a complaint, threatening lawyers or something because China didn't have a properly executed warrant, the fool. The lads are still in Europe, no doubt getting their cocks sucked off in Amsterdam. Been following the tour on local radio, but having lost both games, it doesn't bode well for the new season. Anyhow, Dex didn't go, too busy with work apparently, so I'll go see him tonight, see what info I can get about The Greek, maybe Campbell too.

Andy.

SUNDAY, 19th AUGUST 1984
2055 HOURS
MY FLAT, GLOBE ROAD, STEPNEY

Good night round at Dex's, had a few beers, a few brandys too while he sucked on a cigar, fuck knows when he started puffing on those fucks. Had a few lines of coke too, just a "livener" as he calls it. All the while he's prodding me about what happened with the police, how I ended up getting sacked, do I have any old pals there he could have a chat too, maybe put a bit of work their way. Yeah, China would be up for it for sure, the bent fuck, but I'm not introducing nobody to no-one, nah, I need to keep my different lives apart. I prod him as well, about The Greek and the Millwall crew. Reckons he only knows The Greek vaguely through a friend of a friend, used to buy some cannabis from him but nowadays buys the occasional bag of coke. He put me right on the spot though, asking why I asked, a fucking brilliant question. Why would an ex-police officer ask about current villains? I blurt out a mate on the job is asking if I know of him, there's no harm in me keeping on the right-side of the law. Nodding, he gets it. I'll keep pushing, see what he knows.

Andy.

MONDAY, 20th AUGUST 1984
0805 HOURS
MY FLAT, GLOBE ROAD, STEPNEY

Just had a call from Dex, saying a mate wants a spot of labouring done, few days' work cash in hand. Fuck it, might as well, will keep me busy and provide some welcome funds. Although I get more money after being promoted, plus being TP'd to Inspector, it's roughly the same as I was getting before as plod plus overtime. I'll meet this labouring guy, Trevor, at the end of my road at 0900-hours. Sweet.

Andy.

TUESDAY, 28th AUGUST 1984
1105 HOURS
MY FLAT, GLOBE ROAD, STEPNEY

Away game at Liverpool yesterday, weird having a game on the Bank Holiday. We planned to get the train up there, so met the lads at Euston at 1000-hours. On the concourse, Bee's handing out vouchers for the train, something about washing up powder giving them away for free. Fuck it, saves the £40 train fare. With about 60 or 70 of us and more on later trains, Will reckons the crew will be a couple hundred strong at least. We had to change at Chester, which is a shit-hole to be fair, then wait ages for a "football special" to take us into Liverpool. Just as we pulled into Lime Street Station, our train is pelted with bricks and bottles, the Liverpool crew were waiting for us. Out of the station concourse, we're ambushed, from behind and from each side, with a crew charging up the stairs in front from the main road outside. Will yells "no-one runs, no-body hides", but, we we're out numbered 3 or 4 to one, so have it lively out to the left, powering through the ugly as fuck scousers standing in our way. A fair few of us end up ploughing into a fancy hotel, until the Scouse scumbags outside fucked off. The coaches to the ground depart from the Liver-building down near the docks, fuck it, we'll walk through the city centre proudly singing "bubbles", couple of hundred hard as fuck hammers, nobody's going to fuck with us. Pulling up at the ground, yet more fighting, but, thankfully, nobody got hurt and we all got in. End up losing 3-nil, which is shit, double, actually treble shit, but, Liverpool are a good team. Got back here about midnight a bit worse for wear, had a good laugh though.

Andy.

SUNDAY, 2nd SEPTEMBER 1984
12 NOON
MY FLAT, GLOBE ROAD, STEPNEY

Fuck me, me head's fucking killing. Had a massive night out last night after yet another away game, this time at Southampton, (won 3-two). Pretty leafy round there, so we end up facing off to the local crew on a primary school playing field. Got stuck in, making sure Bee and Will see me going mental, help build my persona. Back to London at 2120-hours, we head to the Bunker Club. Millwall are there too, so we end up having a drink with them, The Greek, nice as pie, introduces me as "the ex-copper". They're all smiling and shaking hands through puzzled eyes, the thick a fuck "sarf" London dicks. Pulling me to one side, says he knows I've been asking Dex about him, wonders why an ex-copper is so interested. Fuck. I explain a pal on the job is tracking down the Heathrow gang, reckons one of them used to go out with a bird he's knocking off. No problem, he smiles. Have this one on me yeah, my treat. Dickie Campbell, he smiles. Yeah, he did it, fuck me, everyone sarf-of-the-river knows he did it too, him and that sneaky fuck copper, "the priest", the one who's been felt for it. Shit, he's talking about Fairbrother. Anyhow, he laughs, Dickie's long-gone mate, fucked off to Marbella I heard, along with two million quid in cash. Rumour is he's left a load of gold with a gyppo down in Kent, can't sell large amounts in one go so they're smelting it down before drip-feeding it through. Right, right, I nod along, not showing much interest. Fucking-hell, he pats me on the back, I though the filth had more about them. Yeah, I agree, fucking clueless. However, this is literally gold-dust, I must report back asap.

Andy.

MONDAY, 3rd SEPTEMBER 1984
0725 NOON
MY FLAT, GLOBE ROAD, STEPNEY

Got another few days labouring lined up, an extension to a house near Victoria Park, not far from here. Digging the foundations, I'll be humping a load of soil into a skip no doubt. Even though I've been ringing Hughes pretty regularly, I start my formal reporting-in from this week, visiting a nick of my choice to give a statement. If I'm still labouring, I'll tell them I have to go sign-on and deal with the DSS fools, or something. If I get spotted, I'll say I've been stopped in my motor and got a producer. Called Hughes yesterday, told him what The Greek told me. Like a pig in shit, says it confirms his theory about Campbell and where the gold might be. Reckons the place in Kent must be the gaff we watched a while back when tracking the gold Rolls Royce, the smelter is suspected to be based there. I asked him about "the priest" and whether this was Fairbrother. While he wouldn't comment, his tone suggests I was spot on. Fuck me, Fairbrother, it's always the quiet ones. Anyhow, he's asked I target The Greek, so at least I know my next task.

Andy.

FRIDAY, 21st SEPTEMBER 1984
2155 HOURS
MY FLAT, GLOBE ROAD, STEPNEY

Just got back, tucking into a kebab. Finished work at midday, as normal on a Friday, had a few pints with the chaps then met up with Dex for a few more pints plus a few lines to keep me sharp. Bumped into Bee down at Silvertown, he's boo-hooing about last week and the debacle at Chelsea. Yeah, we got our arses handed to us on and off the pitch, probably down to Will and his shit planning. The chaps are heading into town for a big night but I've diverted here, suggesting money's tight, with me labouring here and there, cash in hand. Truth is though, I'm really tired, labouring isn't for me, nah, I don't want to be lumbering bags of soil around, plus, it's difficult to report-in 2-weekly, even more difficult to go training. Dex reckons I should pack it all in and become a driver for him, not like a chauffeur or nothing, nah, just moving cars around his couple of lots and running a few errands. Yeah, I'll defo go for it, just don't want to seem too keen. For now, it's a wank, shower, then bed.

Andy.

WEDNESDAY, 26th SEPTEMBER 1984
2155 HOURS
MY FLAT, GLOBE ROAD, STEPNEY

Just back from the gym, weights session plus 30 mins on a heavy bag followed by a few rounds of light sparring. Really enjoyed it actually, yeah, those long sparing sessions way back when with uncle Tommy and cousin Kenny came flooding back. Come to think of it, I haven't been to see him in ages, difficult now he is up near Norwich, must make the effort though. So, I've agreed with Dex to do some driving for him, monkey a week, way better than labouring.

Andy.

SATURDAY, 20th OCTOBER 1984
0900 HOURS
MY FLAT, GLOBE ROAD, STEPNEY

What a week. Been really busy, haven't wrote for a while neither. I've agreed with Hughes to knock the 2-weekly statements on the head, just not realistic and could arouse suspicion. Dex has me moving cars from one place to another, then back again, collecting a few small debts too, nothing heavy, just light intimidation. However, yesterday, he asks me to drop 5-grand round to The Greek. Excellent. I trundle south through the Shadwell Tunnel to a Taxi Office on Southwark Park Road, Bermondsey, fuck me, it's grim around there. I park opposite a pub called the Lion's Den, with a huge union jack with a Millwall club crest hanging in the window. Thank fuck I'm in Dex's Ford Cortina, not my motor, the little toe-rags around there will have the wheels off in 5-seconds flat. Walking in, The Greek's sitting there along with a few heavy looking guys, all smoking resin and looking moody. Chatting for maybe 30 minutes, it's all good, other than being eyeballed by a huge black guy with a fuck off scar across his forehead. Stuffing the envelop bulging with cash into The Greeks fat hand, he hands me larger package, bound up with grey gaffer tape. Following me outside, he passes me a scrap of paper with his number on, says if I want a proper job, doing the doors or something, let him know. Hughes will be impressed.

Andy.

TUESDAY, 25th DECEMBER 1984
1120 HOURS
MY FLAT, GLOBE ROAD, STEPNEY

What a year. I haven't written for ages actually, too fucked. Off to see me mum and dad in a while, christmas dinner and all that, but, fucking hell, don't much feel like eating, stomach's churning, got the shits too. Had a right old night of it last night at a skanky club in Dalston, met The Greek there actually, then, later on, on his recommendation we get a taxi down to the Isle of Dogs, a tower-block right near the Thames for a £30 session with Lisa, (stunning hairdresser by day, filthy Tom by night). Surprised he was into Toms though, says it's cheaper than plying some random bird with drinks all night or going home alone and bashing one out. Yeah, I get that. Got back here at around 0600-hours, and, with about 4 hours kip, I'm literally fucked. Tottenham away tomorrow, those fucking Yids are getting fucked, just like that dirty bitch last night.

Jones.

FRIDAY, 28th DECEMBER 1984
1100 HOURS
MY FLAT, GLOBE ROAD, STEPNEY

A blinding sleep, thank god, I'm exhausted. Been moving shit around for Dex also The Greek, plus doing a few Thursday night doors down at Cheeks in Deptford. On top of that, more nights out with the lads, more home games, more away games, more beers, more curry's, more joints, more speed, more cocaine, more keeping notes, more calling Hughes, more being alert, more listening for names about names, more little rumours here and there, all the while building my criminal persona and keeping the real me hidden. Safe to say I'm fucking exhausted. Also, I'm training like a mad-man, fittest I've ever been actually. Fuck me, can't believe how knackered I am. Roll-on 1985.

Andrew Jones.

TUESDAY, 8th JANUARY 1985
1530 HOURS
MY FLAT, GLOBE ROAD, STEPNEY

Face to face with Hughes today, over at Heston Services out towards Heathrow Airport, poetic really, given our history on the Heathrow job. Basically, he's checking on how I am, reminding me about the PACE regulations and to report any serious wrong-doings. He's happy with the intel I've been providing, football hooliganism and drugs in the main. Still interested in The Greek, of course, and any links he might have to the Heathrow job, he seems especially interested in a new face called "Rude-Boy-Dee". Basic intel suggests he's originally from Brixton but now lives god-knows where, apparently he deals wholesale amounts of drugs, to the likes of the Greek. He's also asked about a guy who knocks around with The Greek called "Tiny", yeah, by his description, I've seen him a few times down at the taxi office in Bermondsey. To be fair, I can take care of myself, but this guy scares the living shit out of me, he's fucking huge. Bee's heard of this "Tiny" fella too, but never actually met him, says he runs a tasty firm as part of the Millwall crew, all of them bouncers across South London, definitely not to be fucked with. Thankfully, Hughes hasn't asked me much about my crew, which is great.

Jones.

WEDNESDAY, 30th JANUARY 1985
1920 HOURS
MY FLAT, GLOBE ROAD, STEPNEY

What a slog. Best part of 4 hours to get back from HMP Norwich, visiting Kenny. Out in the sticks, it's an awful place with huge brown brick walls stinking of sweat and filth, and a fair amount of despair. Funny though, it's on "Knox" Road, as in Fort Knox. Anyhow, looks like Kenny's doing okay, hasn't had much trouble, in fact, although a bit heavier than before, he actually looks quite good, he's even started a course in English Literature, so he says. He's still bitter though, fully intent on revenge when he eventually gets out. Told him about being kicked out of the Met, didn't seem surprised to be fair, says it's for the best, guys like us have no place in the "filth", (his word). No matter how many times he says his fine, enjoying it almost, I know, deep down inside, he's suffering in there.

Jones.

TUESDAY, 5th FEBRUARY 1985
1805 HOURS
MY FLAT, GLOBE ROAD, STEPNEY

Saw The Greek today, fucking hell, he's in a bad way. Millwall faced off with Chelsea yesterday in the FA Cup. On the field, they won 3-2, an amazing result given they are; a) a totally shit team from a shit part of London, and b) they're in the 3rd Division, whereas Chelsea are near the top of the 1st. Off the field, sounds like they spanked Chelsea all over Brompton Cemetery, yeah, fighting in between the gravestones. The police have cracked down on hooligans recently, with a huge presence at the grounds. This pushes the fighting away from the grounds to train station concourses, shopping centres, kids playing fields, and, now, a cemetery, for fucks sake. The Greek's nursing what looks to be a broken nose and a black eye with a few grazes across is head too, but, turns out, the Chelsea top-boy, Tommy McDowell, got seven bells of shit kicked out of him and is currently in intensive care. Apparently, The Greek sparked him out, then, once on the ground, no end of Millwall put the boot in. Rule number one in hooligan fighting, never, (and I mean never-ever), go to the floor. I'll let Hughes know just in case.

Jones.

FRIDAY, 1st MARCH 1985
1810 HOURS
MY FLAT, GLOBE ROAD, STEPNEY

This year's flying by, holy shit. Really busy with Dex as well as keeping close to The Greek. Dex is just a ponce really, selling medium weight to a few pals, small-fry, not dealing in any serious money. The Greek, on the other hand, is a serious bit of work. He runs his distribution operation from the Taxi Office in Bermondsey, the proceeds of which he uses to fund various criminal ventures such as robberies, (post offices mainly), a few prostitutes around South East London, and, of course, the Millwall hooligan crew. He also has a couple of proper security guarding businesses registered at Companies House as well as a coach works around the corner from South Bermondsey train station. Anyway, me and The Greek are sweet, even though we've both agreed our crews need to face each other for a "straightener" sooner rather than later. He reckons I should buy into his business and set up a "shop", (as he calls it), over in the East End. Says there's really only one guy over here wholesaling coke, and he'll be pretty easy to move in on. I'll be doing some research on this fella they call "Obi-Wan", real name Ben, who's pretty old, translating to "old-ben" and then "obi-wan", from Star Wars. For fucks sake, these guys are all pricks. Anyhow, big night out tonight in prep for a huge meet we have tomorrow with the Arsenal.

Andy.

SUNDAY, 3rd MARCH 1985
1540 HOURS
MY FLAT, GLOBE ROAD, STEPNEY

Excellent news, Will is finally out. Had a great couple of days but, fuck me, what a god awful come-down today. Friday night, we head up town intending to go to the Bunker Club but end up in a boozer on Charring Cross Road. From there, we get a taxi up to the Camden Palace for a disco night, absolute carnage. Coke galore, all of us had a right old laugh with a bunch of gay guys and a few of super-fit birds they were hanging out with. Ends up back at some geezers flat in Tottenham where a few of us have a go on a superstar Brazilian looker, (who, in hindsight, may have been a Tom). No doubt I'll be visiting the clap clinic later in the week. Fuck me, need to be sick, need to write about Will though…

Jones.

SUNDAY, 3rd MARCH 1985
1900 HOURS
MY FLAT, GLOBE ROAD, STEPNEY

Fucking hell, god-knows what I took last night, but I'm not right, just puked my guts up. So yesterday, away at Arsenal, we met at Kings Cross station, fucking hundreds of us to be fair. Me, Dex, Bee and of course Will each take a team, making our own way to Highbury to avoid the close attention of the police. Yeah, hopefully we can outflank the Arsenal crew, the "Tribe" they call themselves, mugs, led by a fella called "Connie". Will arranged to meet them on Highbury Fields, an hour before kick-off, so my team sets off marching a 40-minute walk. We get there first, followed by Dex and his team, then Bee and his. In the distance we see red and white scarves and a whole load of noise, the Tribe are approaching. We clash pretty much on the little road running through the Park. Completely out numbering them, smashing them to fuck, their alleged "top boy" Connie was nowhere to be seen. Few minutes later, Will and his team of maybe fifty wander over reckoning they were stopped by no end of police. Bee's not having any of it though, says they've been to the boozer and left us to deal with the Tribe. He and Will have a blazing row with Bee sticking the nut on him before landing a barrage of lightening punches. Will, on his knees, yells for him to stop-stop-stop while we all stand watching in silence, couple hundred of us. Getting up, brushing himself down, he walks off in silence, a sorry sight truth be told. We make it to the ground unscathed, nobody daring to talk about what just went down. Safe to say, Will is now most definitely out.

Jones.

SUNDAY, 3rd MARCH 1985
2310 HOURS
MY FLAT, GLOBE ROAD, STEPNEY

Last thing for today, bumped into Claire last night. Yeah, after the game, we make our way back to the George at Silvertown, having a right laugh about Will. His time had come, plus, Bee well deserves to be top boy. Dex promised to go see Will tomorrow, check he's okay, he's still our mate and more than welcome down at Upton Park. From there, me and Dex head over to Hollywood's at Romford, why the fuck not I say, besides, the crowning of Bee as top boy was beginning to jar. Soon as we get to the bar, we're surrounded by a load of Essex-girl slags, one of them being Claire. Buying her a drink, we have a few laughs then one thing leads to another, before I know it, we're in the toilets snorting coke while I take her from behind. Eventually, we end up back at hers, where I smash the granny out of her and she rides me red-raw. Running up to Harwich tomorrow to pick up a chap called Dave, as a favour for The Greek. I think this might be him testing me, seeing if he can defo trust me, we'll see. Off to bed now.

Jones.

TUESDAY, 5th MARCH 1985
0930 HOURS
MY FLAT, GLOBE ROAD, STEPNEY

What a day. Five hours in the car up to Harwich to pick up "David", a foot passenger returning from Rotterdam. Turns out, he's a courier, of sorts, ferrying a load of cash out to Europe, paying for a delivery of coke due to arrive here in a few days time. A young-looking guy, maybe early twenties, he's confident and steady with a certain maturity and composure about him. We have a good chat and he tells me about growing up in Brixton, then asks me about being a copper. Turns out David's real name is Delroy, otherwise known as Rude-Boy-Dee, (yes, "the" rude-boy-dee Hughes was asking about ages ago). I try teasing-out some details about The Greek or his contacts in Europe, but, he either knows jack shit or is pretty skilled at dodging questions. All I really learnt was a) he defo doesn't work for The Greek, he says he's a mug but is a good buyer who takes a heavy volume of gear and b) works directly for a guy in England, but deals with a firm in Belgium. Dropping him around to The Greeks place in Bermondsey, they're both smiles, handshakes and hugs, both fake as fuck. I'll pass his name, description plus what he told me over to Hughes so he can do some digging.

Jones.

SATURDAY, 9th MARCH 1985
1540 HOURS
MY FLAT, GLOBE ROAD, STEPNEY

Spent yesterday afternoon with The Greek, becoming a bit of bore actually, he's on-and-on about me taking over Obi-Wan's business, (real name, Ben Dunning, according to Hughes). Turns out he does indeed run the cocaine business in East London, has done so since the late seventies but recently has been involved in a turf-war with a Turkish firm in Tottenham about this new "Crack" drug everyone's talking about. The Greek says he's heard Obi-Wan wants an out, feeling vulnerable after the trouble with the Turks and all that, so he's set up a meet between me and Ben next week. Anyhow, after seeing The Greek, I meet the chaps at Silvertown. Turns out Dex has heard of Ben, Bee too, they both reckon he's a serious piece of work not to be fucked with and will definitely resist any attempt to move in on his business. I'll bounce all this off Hughes, feels like I'm getting too close to the legal/illegal line.

Jones.

TUESDAY, 12th MARCH 1985
1855 HOURS
MY FLAT, GLOBE ROAD, STEPNEY

Met with Hughes, floated the idea of moving in on Ben and his business. Wasn't immediately up for it, but, after some chewing it over, says he can see some upside in controlling the flow of supply, while getting more knowledge of the importation routes and those higher up in the organisation, saying smashing the network might be a good exit route for me. He's not sure about the legalities, or whether the higher-uppers will have the balls for it, the fucking pricks. Well, approve it or not, I'm doing it. I need to move up the food chain, no point in fishing in the local pond, yeah, got to start hunting Great Whites, what's the point otherwise.

Jones.

SUNDAY, 17th MARCH 1985
1510 HOURS
MUM AND DADS, RUSCOE ROAD, CANNING TOWN

At the folks gaff, can't go home, not today. Just got off the blower to Hughes, he's ringing me back. It's all gone to shit this week. Wednesday, me, Bee and Will plus about 30 hardcore meet at St Pancras for a train up to Nottingham. Thirty minutes after we set off Bee gets up, this is us, he says as the train pulls into Luton. Luton, what the fuck? Millwall are playing Luton in the FA Cup today, this isn't for us, we're away at Forest. Finding a local boozer, we get a little boisterous with some locals, nothing heavy, just laughs. Few hours later, outside the ground, we clash with Millwall and Luton, teaching them both a lesson, didn't see The Greek though or even that Tiny fella, which was disappointing. Bee produces a bunch of match tickets and we make our way inside. Boring-as-fuck, like watching two kids teams, mid-way through the first half we hear Arsenal, Tottenham and Chelsea chants. What the fuck, this isn't just a ninja-visit behind enemy lines, this is a pre-planned multi-sided war. Kicking off proper, Bee is immense, Will's on form too while I try keeping a low profile, but, I end up getting dragged in. Yeah, a fucking uniformed pleb grabs me, yelling I'm nicked. I tell him I'm working and to fuck off, but, the cunt cracks me over the head. Chinning him, legs folding, he crumples like a sack of shit. Will, the fucking idiot, rips a seat out and smashes it over a numpty copper who collapses. Fighting our way outside, then down the terraced-house streets, we eventually find the train station. Got back to London at midnight, fucked. Hold up, phone's ringing…

Jones.

SUNDAY, 17th MARCH 1985
1535 HOURS
MUM AND DADS, RUSCOE ROAD, CANNING TOWN

That's Hughes, giving me an almighty bollocking for the midweek Luton thing, and the shitstorm yesterday. Tells me I got to make a formal statement on Monday. So, yesterday, The Greek picks me up just after 1700-hours and we drive to Epping Forrest where we find this old pub called "The Oak". Heading around the back we see a "Winkle and Crab" shack with two powerlifter types either side of the door who nod, like we're expected. Showing us inside, we find Ben. He's fucking old alright, easy 50, maybe older, with long grey hair in a ponytail and a dirty white vest. I count six heavy looking blokes around the edge of the room, each giving us the evil eye, the fucking dicks. We have a chit-chat with the arrogant old fuck, well, The Greek does, got the gift of the gab hasn't he. Old Ben says, in no uncertain terms, he has absolutely no interesting in any partners, or indeed selling the business, no matter how much is on offer, or whatever protection I, or anyone in the police can offer. Fine, understood, The Greek sighs, before leaving. Walking back to the car, he's fuming, says we should fuck Ben and his bodybuilder pricks. Opening the boot, he pulls out a sawn-off shotgun. Right, he shouts, lets fucking have it. Fuck. Back to the shack, without saying a word, he shoots the guy on the left in the leg, who screams out in pain while the other guy, (a pussy), drops to his knees, with his hands out, "p-p-p-please don't shoot." Then, the door flings open and Ben's standing legs astride, face screwed up. The Greek aims right at him, straightener, he shouts, right here, right now. Phone again, hang on…

Jones.

SUNDAY, 17th MARCH 1985
1605 HOURS
MUM AND DADS, RUSCOE ROAD, CANNING TOWN

It's Hughes again, the scouse twat, saying the higher-uppers have authorised me to proceed gaining control of Bens business, but, with two strict conditions. First, I must take Ben into custody, and second, I must not personally deal or permit the dealing of any drugs, or be in receipt of any proceeds arising from the sale or supply of said drugs, the police can't be seen to be dealing drugs. Fuck off, do they think I'm stupid. So, back to yesterday. Bens whips off his vest, leaps the few steps and is bouncing like a middle-weight boxer. Smiling, The Greek goes to pass me the gun and take his leather jacket off but, I can't let him do this, this is my fight. Fuck me, even at a thousand years old, Ben can fight, yeah he's tough, with a granite chin, he's had training, boxing for sure, maybe judo too. After fuck knows how long rolling on the floor, I mount him and start pounding his head. Then, somehow locking my arm up, he spins us over, but, I'm a dirty street fighting cunt, so with my other arm, I punch the cunt in the balls maybe 10 times, then, I'm up, kicking the shit out of him. He's curled up on the floor and the bodybuilders edge forward. Loading another cartridge, The Greek tells them to fuck off and for me to grab Ben. Walking backwards toward the car, I fling Ben in the boot, then, wheels spinning we have it away. The Greek's got him at a lock-up in Bermondsey, I'm due down there tomorrow. I can't go home just in case, hence why I'm with the folks.

Jones.

TUESDAY, 19th MARCH 1985
2130 HOURS
CLAIRES HOUSE, EXMOUTH ROAD, WALTHAMSTOW

Good news, Ben's now in custody, so, it's official, a serving Metropolitan Police officer now controls the wholesale cocaine business in East London. Fucking tough going though. Arriving at the lock up, I find Ben stripped naked, beaten to fuck and tied to a chair with his feet in a bucket of water and a 12-volt car battery clipped to his right hand. The Greek stands over him, holding the other clip precariously over his shoulder. Handing me a claw-hammer, he says today's the day I get to choose what life I want to lead. Too fucking right it is. I'm ashamed to say I hit poor old Ben a couple dozen times, with the handle, not the head, (I'm not a complete monster). Eventually, he says he'll let me have the business, only if I guarantee him an "out". While I didn't make any firm commitments, I'm not the law, remember, I tell him I've still got pals on the job, so I'll try my best. 5 minutes later, he gives up his wholesale contact, "Valentine", says he'll call him to tell him what happened and hand over the business. What the fuck is it with these guys and their nick-names? He also gives me the names and addresses of his main dealers, seven of them to be precise, says each of these has a team of street dealers who punt the stock. Mate, this is way too fucking easy, these guys are pricks.

Jones.

FRIDAY, 22nd MARCH 1985
1830 HOURS
MY FLAT, GLOBE ROAD, STEPNEY

Things are moving quickly. Had a call from this "Valentine" character earlier in the week, says he's heard of me, acknowledged Ben's out and I'm in, says it's part and parcel of the business, every story has an ending. Giving me chapter and verse about how the business works, says my contact is Rude-Boy-Dee and, if I acquire cocaine or any other drug from anywhere else, it'll not end well. Yeah, we'll see about that, you fucking ponce. Can't actually believe Dee supplied both Ben and The Greek, yet neither of them were aware. Straight after that call, Dee calls, says he'll deliver direct to Bens team, who are now my team, they'll punt the shit out and deliver the cash to me. Says I have to then pay him, no matter what, and to listen to what Valentine says, that any fucking around would result in complete carnage, he's not a guy to cross. Day after, I tour around to see Bens, sorry, my dealers, tell them what's expected of them and make sure they're on board. Also, I had yet another briefing with Hughes, giving me the "rules of engagement". I cannot knowingly commit any crime nor be participant to the planning of any such crime, plus, I cannot physically deal or knowingly permit the dealing of drugs, nor receive, benefit or pass-on any proceeds of any such crime. The fucking pleb, how on earth am I going to make this work otherwise, fucking dickhead-yah.

Jones.

FRIDAY, 31st MAY 1985
2137 HOURS
MY FLAT, GLOBE ROAD, STEPNEY

What a month, in fact, what a year. Haven't wrote for ages, just been too busy, I'm fucking drained. Bens cocaine business is a piece of piss, my real role, as it turns out, is to keep the peace between rival networks, such as The Greeks, ward-off any jonny-come-lately wanna-bees while chasing up Bens/my team, who manage a load of street-dealers. Twice a week, collecting the take, I deduct Dee's share of 50%, then, with the remainder, I declare half to Hughes and store the other half under the floorboards in the bathroom. It all works surprisingly well actually, almost like a legit business would. On the West Ham front, Bee and the chaps are well and truly fucked, yeah, Hughes told me of a new, deep-cover op focusing on hooliganism, especially with the fall-out from all the madness in Belgium with the Liverpool fans. Fucking hell, having a fight between consenting adults to prove who's the top team, yeah, I get that, but when dozens of innocent fans needlessly die, mate, that's disgusting. I've told the chaps to calm the fuck down, but, Bee in particular, aint ever having that.

Jones.

SUNDAY, 29th SEPTEMBER 1985
1810 HOURS
MY FLAT, GLOBE ROAD, STEPNEY

Listen yeah, a storm is coming. Demand for product is increasing and, as a result, I'm banking about 5-grand a week, way up from the 2 to 3 when I first started. I've really got to find somewhere to store this cash, can't keep it all here. Turns out, a lady got shot in Brixton yesterday and the riots have started again, just like they did back in '81. Brought it all back to be fair, made me think about my life since and what I'm actually doing with it. Sure, I'm passing more and more info to Hughes, and, a few guys have been picked up as a result, like Ben, but, as soon as they are, another little shit steps up to take their place. We'll never win this war fighting it like we are, no chance.

Jones.

SUNDAY, 7th OCTOBER 1985
2210 HOURS
MY FLAT, GLOBE ROAD, STEPNEY

Got to be quick, gathering some things then heading to Claires, (we're back on by the way, have been for ages now). The whole city is up in flames with a fucking massive riot yesterday at The Farm in Tottenham, otherwise known as the Broadwater Farm estate. The whole area, along with most of North London is controlled by a Jamaican called "Sam", a huge dealer of everything and anything, weed, heroin coke and, mainly, crack-cocaine. We've had a few run-ins with Sam's crew, but, to be fair to him, they've tended to keep their distance. I'm not too worried to be honest, The Greek tells me Sam's busy fighting mini-wars with a firm from Brixton and a firm over in Harlesden, North West London over who sells crack. Apparently, crack is mad-addictive and massively profitable too, but, Valentine isn't into it, too "urban" for him apparently, the prick. Back to The Farm, saw on the news a copper's been killed up there, now, that's serious shit, hence why I'm going to ground for a few weeks. I can't imagine what his family or teammates are going through. To be honest, it's sort of brought me back to who I am and what my real objectives are. I'm a copper, first and foremost, something I've sort of lost sight of recently. Due to the murder of a serving officer, Hughes and the higher-uppers might well pull all COG10 deep-cover officers in, maybe even divert everyone into tracking whoever did it. I can't be brought in, not yet, not right now, my cover would be blown to fuck, ruining all my hard work.

Jones.

SATURDAY, 2nd NOVEMBER 1985
0935 HOURS
MY FLAT, GLOBE ROAD, STEPNEY

Off to meet Hughes, in person, at Paddington Green nick. Yeah, after yesterday's events, I've got to make an official statement, apparently. So I'm invited down to Braintree for Dex's wedding, he's been seeing Sue since secondary school, it's about time he did the right thing. I didn't fancy no church do, nah, so met them at a fancy gaff called Gosfield Hall, north of Braintree, for the reception. Claires all dolled up and sexy and I'm looking rather dapper too, even if I say so myself. We're actually having a good time, moving and grooving on the dancefloor when a little wanna-be bumps into us. Not to worry, we've all had a drink and a sniff, it's a busy place yeah. Swinging around, he's pointing at his now beer splattered shirt, giving me verbals. One thing leads to another, the cunt gets a slap and skids across the dancefloor, funny really. Claire's screaming at me to leave him alone and I see Dex scrambling to get at us, but, the little shit's back on his feet, guard up, goading me, giving it the big-un. Crowd parting, music fading out, mate, it's tense. PC Andrew Jones would pacify the situation, calm it all down, but, what would Jones, the ICB nutcase and east-end king of coke do? 10 minutes later, I'm in the back of Bee's Range Rover, heading back to London while I get bollock naked. Crawling through to the boot, I grab his gym bag and slip on his Fred Perry shorts and 10-seasons old replica West Ham top. Says there's too many witnesses so he'll burn my clothes later after dropping me home. Not sure if the little mug is dead, in any case, it's defo GBH, if not attempted murder. Called Hughes to let him know, he's fucking on one, hence the face to face.

Jones.

TUESDAY, 12th NOVEMBER 1985
2335 HOURS
MY FLAT, GLOBE ROAD, STEPNEY

Hughes got back to me today about the wedding, no further action will be taken, thank fuck. The little mug is okay, although he's still in hospital under police guard. The cunt took a beating and a half, yeah, if I'm honest, for a split second, I lost control and I didn't like that feeling. Giving me a bollocking for letting it get out of hand, he asks if I'm losing perspective, if I still know where the line is. It's a good question, but, of course I fucking do, the fucking dick, he's getting right on my tits. He suggests I meet with a contact he refers to as "Seven-Bravo", meaning he's a fellow deep-cover officer, for me to give him an insight into football hooliganism. He's arranged for us to meet in Hastings, on the South Coast, and asked me to travel on public transport too in order to minimise the risk of being followed. Fair do's, I get it.

Jones.

SUNDAY, 17th NOVEMBER 1985
1105 HOURS
MY FLAT, GLOBE ROAD, STEPNEY

So, met this guy yesterday in Hastings at the pub on the corner, opposite the train station. Fuck me, he can talk, talk-talk-talk. Tubby little fella, wouldn't say boo to a goose, he's shy on detail but I gather he's embedded into the Millwall crew. He's firing loads of shit questions about The Greek and his buddy "Tiny", also Bee and, oddly, Dex. Forty minutes later, with a friendly handshake we agree to keep in touch, both knowing full well that's unlikely. Fuck knows what he really wanted, or why Hughes wanted me to meet him in the first place, maybe he'll report back to Hughes, giving him a view on me, what I'm about, whether I've gone rogue and all that bollocks. One thing is certain though, should our paths cross again, deep cover or not, I'll fucking do for the Millwall mug.

Jones.

FRIDAY, 20th DECEMBER 1985
1844 HOURS
MY FLAT, GLOBE ROAD, STEPNEY

Interesting chat with Dex today. Told him I've heard a rumour from a friend of a friend, a serving copper, that the police are asking questions about him. Nodding along, he's got a weird smile on his face, I wonder if he knows I'm still on the job. Yeah, he didn't seem phased by me tipping him the wink, so, I got to wonder. Chit-chatting while he rolls a joint, he offers me some good advice about how to deal with my cash, suggesting I buy property, residential houses and rare sports cars too as these tend to increase in value and can be bought below "book-value" in the right circumstances, meaning I can "sell" higher and officially bank a tidy profit. He also suggests I buy into "cash" businesses, such as bookies or laundrettes where it's easy to flush cash through into the banking system, that's smart. Yeah, come the day of the Grand National, instead of banking the real £20-grand taken through the tills, what do you know, we've had a blinder and actually taken £40, nice, clean and legal. Reckons engaging a cute accountant is essential, and has given me the details of his guy based in Stamford Hill. As always, any advice from Dex about business is good advice.

Jones.

WEDNESDAY, 1st DECEMBER 1985
1035 HOURS
MY FLAT, GLOBE ROAD, STEPNEY

No big New Years Eve for me, nah, turns out being an infamous drug dealer is a lonely life. Watching my back constantly, all the fit birds on the manner are scared to be around me, even Claire doesn't want to know any more, ever since Dex's wedding and my monstering of that little shit-cunt. We'd kind of run our course anyway I reckon, every story has an ending and all that. Can't even enjoy my beloved West Ham no more, it's more about Bee playing cat-and-mouse with the police, hell-bent in stopping all hooligan trouble. Truth be told, I sort of miss my old life, miss my wife too, if I'm honest. Fuck me, never in a million years did I think I might actually miss her, the moody-steady-as-she-goes-moany-fat-cow. Yeah, New Years is shit.

Andrew Jones.

SATURDAY, 1st FEBRUARY 1986
1055 HOURS
MY FLAT, GLOBE ROAD, STEPNEY

The year's started with a bang, quite literally, yeah, got fucking shot at during the week. Just rolls of the tongue nowadays, doesn't worry me, it's just one of those things I suppose. How the fuck is it that an attempt on my life is just "one of those things". Went to visit a fucking dickhead called Paulo, who runs a flat for me on the Beaconstree Estate, Dagenham. To be fair, he punts a fair amount of product around there and is pretty much always on time with his cash plus, he keeps a lid on any locals stepping out of line. Anyhow, after collecting the cash and sharing a joint, I'm getting into my motor when a grey Ford Sierra screeches around the corner. Shit. Back window wound down, 2 shots are fired, one hitting the passenger door, one ricocheting off the wall behind me. Leaping into the motor, I spin the wheels but, by then, the fucking mugs have had it away, the cheeky cunts. Paulo is out of the front door ranting and raving, telling me he'll find out who it was then deal with them. All mouth, but we'll see.

Jones.

WEDNESDAY, 5th FEBRUARY 1986
2130 HOURS
MY FLAT, GLOBE ROAD, STEPNEY

Fucking hate Hughes, the cunt.

Jones.

THURSDAY, 6th MARCH 1986
1000 HOURS
MY FLAT, GLOBE ROAD, STEPNEY

Not wrote for a fair while, busy doing nothing I suppose. Still passing Hughes whatever info I have, mainly about the dealer network, but, he's pushing hard for more information on "Valentine" so I arranged a meet with Rude-Boy-Dee yesterday, I actually like the kid. Headed down to Dover, at his request, a "flying visit" he called it. Met at a quant guest house on the Esplanade, docks on the left, marina on the right and France 20-odd miles away out in the distance. Plate of sandwiches and a mug of tea each, we chit-chat about the business. For a younger guy, he's got an old head on his shoulders, well-educated too, he doesn't sound like an inner-city sink-estate kid. Using my training, I try getting more out of him about Valentine and his contacts in Europe. Vague as ever, says Valentine's a business-man with fingers in loads of pie's, not just drugs, but all sorts before replaying his standard line of don't fuck with this guy, he's seriously connected. As for Europe, he's a bit more open, almost boasting, says he deals with a crew originally from Holland who now base themselves in a shit-hole called Molenbeek, Belgium, who have links with the Middle East. Says he's been all over on business, Milan, Tbilisi, Bucharest, the desert too, taking a flight to Turkey, then a day's drive south. Of course, I'll embellish all this when I pass it on to Hughes, yeah, he'll be like a dog with 2 dicks, spunking all over Interpol or something.

Jones.

FRIDAY, 7th MARCH 1986
1730 HOURS
MY FLAT, GLOBE ROAD, STEPNEY

Fucking hell, just back from the gym where a ponce only tries to sell me, yes ME, drugs, the cheeky bastard. I'm pounding out some serious benches, lifting nearly 200kgs when this muscle-bound-freak wanders up, no neck, bulging biceps, clearly doesn't know who I am. Whispers he can help me achieve "maximum gains", something about being mesomorphic. How so, I ask. Says I've got good genetics, so a couple of injections per week would do it, £50 a go. To be fair, if it's not complete bullshit, sounds like a winner, although, I do hate needles.

Jones.

SUNDAY, 9th MARCH 1986
2254 HOURS
MY FLAT, GLOBE ROAD, STEPNEY

Great weekend, best in a long while. Met the lads down at Silvertown, tends to be the only place I don't instantly get recognised, which is great. Bee and Dex were in good form, as too Will, who's settled into his elder-statesman role nicely. We have some sniff, a few drinks and end up with a curry down at Mile End. Feels almost normal, like old-old times, didn't realise how much I missed my old carry-on. They're my oldest mates, mates before the police and before cocaine, true mates. Bee reckons it's harder and harder to get meets with other firms nowadays, says the police are all over the scene now with rumours of a special task force, even whispers of under-cover sleeper-cells infiltrating firms. Fuck me, my arse got a bit twitchy when that particular topic of convo came up. With the Hammers doing well in the league, they've roped me into an away game at Chelsea at the end of the month. Oh yes.

Jones.

FRIDAY, 28th MARCH 1986
2335 HOURS
MY FLAT, GLOBE ROAD, STEPNEY

Spent the day with Rude-Boy-Dee, says he needs to cool-it with Europe for a while, they've had a spot of internal fighting and "reorganisation" to contend with. Noting my face drop, he goes on to say, with a smile, our supply line shouldn't be affected and for me to stay cool, but, we should begin to tell the network there might be shortages, preparing punters for higher prices. Says as soon as we do this, demand will go through the roof, so we must be ready to cut the shit up more and edge the price up week by week. Worrying about stock, I ask him about the other parts of London and whether he supplies to them too. Smiling, says he's wondered when I'll get round to asking. Says deep south is split between The Greek and the Yardies from Brixton, but nowadays they're more into crack than just powder, so, as long as they don't step on each other toes, it's cool. Says he's nothing to do with the Yardie's, they get supply from the Caribbean and New York City, besides, they're bad payers, cause too much trouble and can't be trusted. He goes onto say West and North West London are dominated by Turkish gangs, mainly into skagg, supplied direct from North Africa apparently, via Spain. Like an encyclopaedia of dealing, if he's not directly involved, he sure knows a lot about the trade. I'll tip Hughes the wink, might get him off my back for a while. Off to bed soon, big day tomorrow with the "Chelsea smilers", what a name, the fucking twats.

Jones.

SUNDAY, 30th MARCH 1986
1455 HOURS
MY FLAT, GLOBE ROAD, STEPNEY

Great day yesterday. Bee arranged for a top-team meet at Trafalgar Square at 1100-hours, way before the police would be on alert, and, far away from any football ground and any specialist riot police. Taking the tube to Westminster then walking up Whitehall, we're there first, about 40 of us. A while later, we hear the Chelsea, "Chelsea-Chelsea" they chant approaching from the east, coming down the Strand. Steaming in, it's over pretty quick with Bee dominating from the front. I smash a couple of chancers but half their crew ran off as soon as the fighting starts, the mugs. Not us though, nah, this is our top team, we stand firm. As for the game, we won 4-nil, we're right up there near the top of the league. Can't really think about winning the league yet, but, who knows.

Jones.

SUNDAY, 30th MARCH 1986
1515 HOURS
MY FLAT, GLOBE ROAD, STEPNEY

Forgot to mention, after the match we headed back into town to a new gaff called the "Shining-Light", an old church on Shaftsbury Avenue, not far from our old place, the Bunker Club. By pure fluke, we bump into The Greek and his boys, they had a home game with local rivals Charlton. Everyone respectful and calm, it's pretty relaxed in there. Way after midnight, maybe 0200-hours, The Greek suggests we go find a Tom, (he loves Tom's). Well, I say, as it happens, I used to know a Tom not far from here, a small place off Wardour Street. Leaving the troops having a right laugh, we stroll through Soho towards Tylers Court, but, it's all boarded up. To be honest, a little bit of me hoped I might see Maisey there, haven't thought about her for years to be honest. The Greek then marches us around to Old Compton Street then up some stairs above a Chinese restaurant with a handwritten sign saying "Sports Massage" pinned on the frame of the door. Top of the stairs there's a locked door painted red with an intercom next to it. Quick buzz and the door unlocks. Inside, we're led into separate rooms, dimly lit with a massage table inside. 2 small geisha looking jap girls walk in wearing traditional robes who gesture for me to get undressed then lay on the table. They pour warm oil all over my chest, massaging the shit out of me before I explode all over them. Pricey, but the best £200 I've spent in a long time.

Jones.

SATURDAY, 7th APRIL 1986
1030 HOURS
MY FLAT, GLOBE ROAD, STEPNEY

Getting ready for the gym, fuck me, I'm fucking tired, yeah, I'll do a few lines before I go, these late nights are playing havoc with my training schedule. Out with Dex last night, he came with me on a collection route, Walthamstow then Isle of Dogs then over to Dagenham. He's sorted me a new motor, a lovely dark grey 2.8 litre Capri, it's the bollocks. I could have bought a Porsche or Ferrari, but this would only ever draw attention, a magnet for keen-as-mustard coppers or wanna-be villains. He's asking a lot of questions about the cash we're collecting and the business in general, when, bolt from the blue, he asks whether I'm still a copper or "on the payroll" as he calls it. Shit. While he's hinted at it before, he hasn't asked outright so I'm not sure whether he's fishing for details or if he actually knows something. In terms of the cash, I told him I'm pocketing £5-grand a week, after expenses, (expenses being 50% to Valentine via Rude-Boy-Dee and 25% to Her Majesty via the Met Police.) Reality is, I'm banking way more than that, but I'm not telling him shit. Some quick maths, he reckons I'll have best part of a quarter to half a mill stashed away. Wow, I've never counted it, never really thought of it like that. He reminds me about getting an accountant, which, thinking about it, are wise words actually.

Jones.

FRIDAY, 4th JULY 1986
2305 HOURS
MY FLAT, GLOBE ROAD, STEPNEY

Haven't been home this early on a Friday night for fuck knows how long, haven't wrote anything in months neither. I got to get a grip. Rude-Boy-Dee called earlier saying Samuel, the top guy from Tottenham wants to meet, talk business. I've been at this now for more than a year so a meet at this point feels odd, suspicious almost. Dee suggests an Italian in Walthamstow, it'll be booked out all night for just us with both firms being jointly responsible of security, which sounds like a recipe for carnage. I'll go along though, hear him out at the very least, maybe get some interesting info for Hughes.

Jones.

TUESDAY, 8th JULY 1986
1500 HOURS
MY FLAT, GLOBE ROAD, STEPNEY

Met with Bee, yeah he's up for security on Saturday. Thought about using some of old Bens crew, that dickhead Paulo would be good for it, he's idiot enough to jump in front of a bullet no doubt, but, I completely trust Bee. Says he'll use a dozen or so guys who do the doors at Southend, rather than any local-local guys who might have a connection to Tottenham. I haven't told Hughes, the twat, nah, he'll probably want me wearing a microphone, or have the place wired up with CCTV, might even want to do a snatch operation and take Samuel out. Nah, I'll ride this one alone, see how it plays out.

Jones.

WEDNESDAY, 9th JULY 1986
1605 HOURS
MY FLAT, GLOBE ROAD, STEPNEY

Just back from a meeting with the accountant Dex recommended, a dodgy as fuck Yid based in Stamford Hill. I explain I'm an entrepreneur with several businesses on the go, so would rather not pay tax. Laughing, says, we all have to pay tax, that's a certainty in life, but, ensuring we pay the right amount of tax, is the key. Yeah, I like him already. He agrees investing in property is good business but says with a nod and a wink "development" rather than acquisition will be more tax efficient. He suggests investment in foreign schemes provides greater returns, but, presents more risk. Yeah, I get it, he's wanting me to invest in downtown Tel-a-fucking-Viv or somewhere, then just after me handing over my cash, bingo, there appears to be a problem with the local government or whoever the fuck, and I've lost all my loot. Yeah, he can fuck off, do the books and give me advice for sure, but, any aggro, I'll end the Yiddish fucker.

Jones.

SATURDAY, 12th JULY 1986
0855 HOURS
MY FLAT, GLOBE ROAD, STEPNEY

Had dinner last night with Samuel. Nice enough guy I suppose, but man, it was hard work. Yeah, he's weighing me up, testing whether he can step into my world, whether the rumours about me are true. Earlier in the evening, Bee gave me a handgun, for my inside pocket just in case. Browning 9-mill, pretty tasty bit of kit actually. I count seven rounds, clean too, cleaned by a professional by the look of it. I had a decent plate of meatballs, him a lobster pasta thing. After some chit-chat, we agree to respect each other's area and be alert should the Turks from North West try moving East. I think this is his main play, seeking numbers in case the Turks move in on him. I get it, not a bad play to be fair. Turns out he's from South London, not the West Indies as popular belief would have it. Says he was around in the riots, back in '81, and was the run-around for the main dealer on the frontline, an old-school dreadlock guy called Crissy, operating out of the Windsor Pub. Yeah, I remember that place, a shithole as I recall. No trouble at the restaurant, which is good news, afterwards, me and Bee head over to Silvertown for last orders where he mentions a "pre-season" holiday in Amsterdam. You know what, yeah, I'm more than up for it. Been skulking around here for way too long so a bit of football, spot of hooliganism, some tasty Dutch weed and maybe some European pussy will be right up my street.

Jones.

WEDNESDAY, 6th AUGUST 1986
1640 HOURS
MY FLAT, GLOBE ROAD, STEPNEY

Fucking hell, had to wait all day in a shit-hole Government building in Victoria to get a new passport, the one I got as a teenager for the school trip to France expired years back. We're meeting at Bee's place in Canning Town before getting a couple of mini buses up to Harwich for the ferry to Holland, Bee reckons they'll be about 30 of us in total. We have a couple of pre-season games, one against Dynamo Dresden from Germany, who we've heard have a tasty firm, then back to Amsterdam for the weekend, coming home on the Sunday. You know what, I really can't wait, at last something interesting to do. These cocaine dick-splashes are just boring, and giving tittle-tattle to Hughes is a chore, plus, he's a dick. I can't believe I once admired the cunt. Anyhow, roll on Holland and bring on zee-Dutch!

Jones.

SUNDAY, 10th AUGUST 1986
1310 HOURS
MY FLAT, GLOBE ROAD, STEPNEY

So, no Holland then, it's all gone to shit, but, we had a laugh anyway. Unknown to us, (I think), we had Liverpool, Everton and Man U all on the same Ferry. Man U were on their way to play Ajax while Liverpool and Everton had a tournament in Hamburg. It all starts in a bar near the ferry terminal. Yeah, with chants, beer and banter we have a right old laugh, carries on to the Ferry where we have a proper giggle. Then, maybe twenty minutes after departing, a pissed-up Scouse twat gives it large so a Man U dickhead jumps in. They're lumping each other over and over, neither could really fight, it's almost comical to watch. One thing leads to another and we're all in fighting, for fucking ages too I might add. The bar obliterated, claret literally everywhere, we chase the Man U scum all over the ship, bumping into the Liverpool crew while we're at it. After an hour, the captain informs us he's turning back, and the police will be waiting for us at Harwich. Each team withdraws to their own bar, looks like every floor on the ship has one. Approaching the harbour, we see a sea of blue-lights at the ferry terminal. Marching down the gang-plank we're booed by the other passengers, before a few of the boys, including Bee, gets pulled and carted off. The rest of us walk 2 miles back to the train station straight onto a Special back to Liverpool Street. So, no Amsterdam, no European totty to indulge, no Dutch weed to smoke, no Europeans to fuck with, no break from reality. Sad times.

Jones.

WEDNESDAY, 13th AUGUST 1986
1740 HOURS
MY FLAT, GLOBE ROAD, STEPNEY

Fucking hard session at the gym, but it's all paying off. I'm looking pretty fine, even if I say so myself. It needed to be huge, had best part of an hour on the phone to Hughes before leaving. Apparently, up at Harwich, I got caught on camera by the anti-hooligan "Football Task Force", so now the higher-uppers are concerned I might be going rogue. Straight off, they can fuck right off, I'm the one taking all the risks, literally risking my life for these cunts. He's officially warned me to be careful, and wants me to re-sign the PACE bullshit handbook, plus, he wants me to get a transportable phone in case he needs to speak to me at any time. Says a lot of poncy city traders have them and they're only a couple of grand so well within my price-range, (the sarcastic twat). Yeah, I've seen a few guys with them out and about, will give it a go, anything to shut the cunt up.

Jones.

SUNDAY, 7th SEPTEMBER 1986
1900 HOURS
MY FLAT, GLOBE ROAD, STEPNEY

Day off today, did a bit of sparring. Got a new guy training down there, a tasty chap called Benji Stephens, defo a future world champ middleweight, although, fuck me, he hits like a heavyweight. Going to look at some houses next week with Dex and his missus Sue. They both reckon I should move out of town, buy a bigger place, a proper house, not, as they both put it, a "fuck-hole-bachelor-pad". As for the coke business, steady as she goes, it's running like clockwork. To be fair, it's a piece of piss. I got the whole team portable phones, nifty looking Motorola things with sticky out ariels so that I can call them at any time, keep the dirty fucks on their toes, saves me going to see them in person. I've heard nothing else from Sam up at Tottenham, so I'm assuming everything with the Turks has calmed down. Seen The Greek a fair few times, you know what, I actually like him, he's pretty cool, reckon in a different life we could have been proper mates. Funny, he never fails to remind me our day of destiny will eventually come. Yeah right, the twat.

Jones.

MONDAY, 6th OCTBER 1986
1030 HOURS
MY FLAT, GLOBE ROAD, STEPNEY

Holy shit, it's World War three. Had Bee round here yesterday, ranting and raving, wanting me to get hold of The Greek, threatening he wants to kill him. Just what we need, just when things were settling down too, I can't catch a fucking break around here. Last Saturday, we're away at Watford while Millwall were away to Palace. Bee had arranged a bit of a meet-up with the Millwall at Trafalgar Square, (his favourite meeting place ever since mullering Chelsea earlier in the year). Long story short, other than Bee, it's mostly kids and second tier guys, none of the top table fellas we know. One of the younger lads gets separated and chased, eventually getting stabbed around the back of Charring Cross station, dies on the way to the hospital, the poor bugger. Bee is fucking fuming, losing his head, says he'll do serious time over this, says it's on him, he's to blame, he's got to take matters into his own hands. I tell him I'm sorry about the kid, I really am too, but I can't give him The Greek, there's too much at stake. He goes fucking ballistic, telling me I've changed, that I'm as far from the ICB as I ever have been, and, I'm no friend of his. Boo-fucking-hoo, the fucking big baby.

Jones.

SUNDAY, 19th OCTOBER 1986
1202 HOURS
MY FLAT, GLOBE ROAD, STEPNEY

After seeing fuck knows how many houses, I've actually found one in a place called Frinton, a lovely quiet seaside town. No arcades, no kiss-me-quick hats or hen-do's, nah, this place is classy, shit, I have the golf club literally next door, might even give it a go. The gaff is pricey, but I can afford it, actually, more than afford it. Arry, from Stamford Hill, now my official accountant, suggests I take a mortgage out, rather than paying cash, cash is too obvious apparently, might alert the authorities. He's set up a company, registered in Jersey, where I own 80% of the shares, Dex 10% as he's already a Director of a few other firms which makes getting loans easier to obtain, and Arry, as Company Secretary owns 10% also. We'll trade the cash through the firm, with deposits from the 3 betting shops I'm in the process of buying. The firm will take a mortgage out for the Frinton house and any other I wish to acquire, then, after a couple of years or so, we'll liquidate the firm, pay the mortgages off before disposing of the properties at a discounted rate, to myself of course, or an alternative new-firm we'll set up and start the palaver again. Nice.

Jones.

THURSDAY, 30th OCTOBER 1986
2025 HOURS
MY SECERET HOUSE, CORNER OF SECOND AVENUE AND ESPANADE, FRINTON-ON-SEA

So, here I am in my new monstrosity of a house. 6-bedroom, 4-bathroom, 3-floor mock-tudor bastard overlooking the sea. I love it, best half a million I've ever spent, (ha, that's so funny). Seriously, this will be my get-away pad, I'll keep it secret, travelling up here only now and again, using different routes and all that covert shit. It's an hour and half from London, even quicker actually due to the new M25 motorway, and a 30-minute drive from Colchester. I got a gardener and a cleaner, the previous owner suggests I keep them both on. Yeah, the lady I've bought it from recently lost her husband of 40 years, a retired surgeon I think she said, anyway, she's happy I could complete so quickly, off to live with her daughter, or something. I'll be getting an industrial bank safe installed in the basement, (which is massive by the way), to keep cash in and of course you, my beauty, my diaries, my evidence, my anchor back to reality. For tonight, I'm sleeping on the 4-poster the old dear has left in the master bedroom. Yeah, feel like Henry the fucking 8th!

Jones.

THURSDAY, 6th NOVEMBER 1986
1230 HOURS
MY FLAT, GLOBE ROAD, STEPNEY

Retribution and retaliation has started. Last night, at a huge council-run bonfire on Blackheath Common there's a fight and Bee, still on one about the young-un who got killed, stabs one of the Millwall crew in the leg four or five times, severed an artery apparently. The victim works the doors for Tiny, which now means no end of fucking hassle and aggravation. Making a quick getaway, Bee calls me while running through Greenwich Park toward the foot tunnel into the Isle of Dogs where he'll get a taxi, the fucking idiot. Then, an hour or so later, The Greek calls, full of adrenaline and testosterone, ranting and raving. I tell him to calm down and fucking do one, eye for an eye and all that. I'll have to let Hughes know though, yeah, this could end up messy.

Jones.

SUNDAY, 23rd NOVEMBER 1986
1110 HOURS
MY FLAT, GLOBE ROAD, STEPNEY

Fucking hell, big night out last night, was just having my cocked sucked by Racheal or Ruby or whatever the fuck her name is and had to take a call from Dex, says Bee's in hospital with fucking gunshot wounds. Shit. He's doing the doors down at "Juliets" in Southend on Friday night when a group a geezers stroll up. Pissed up drunk and rowdy, after a short scuffle he sends them on their way. Half an hour later, they come back armed with a shooter and spray the door-crew and the queuing punters. A few punters are hit, a couple with shrapnel wounds and one is in a critical condition. Bee's hit too, currently in intensive care having had an operation yesterday. Why the fuck am I only hearing about this now? Dex is convinced it's Millwall, retaliating for the Blackheath stabbing. Woah, slow the fuck down, it's more than likely them, but, and it's a fucking big but, we have zero evidence, the fucking fool. We all need to slow the fuck down otherwise we'll all end up dead or in jail. I'll go see Bee later and call The Greek, try and straighten all this out, but, for now, back to that tidy glistening wet Tom in the bedroom.

Jones.

MONDAY, 24th NOVEMBER 1986
1746 HOURS
MY FLAT, GLOBE ROAD, STEPNEY

Bollocks. Had a roasting this morning from Hughes, giving large about the level of violence increasing, that my deployment is supposed to ease the trouble, yet, there's more violence and more drugs than ever. All they have to show is a few arrests of low to mid-level plebs plus old Ben, which is a really shit return to be fair. But, the main pain in my ass is our flat on Beaconsfield Road, near Star Lane Park. Yeah, got rumbled on Saturday night, and, even worse, I'm only hearing about it today. All the stock has been taken, cash too, plus the fucking dick who runs the shop, a clueless fucker called "Ernest" gets the shit kicked out of him. Reckons the guys who did it were all black, well trained and knew exactly what they were doing, tooled up too with guns, apparently. He's run the shop for a good few years and seems to be well respected, to be fair, I've had no reason to doubt him since taking over. Given the descriptions, they must be part of Sam's crew, yeah, no fucking doubt about it. Why bother with all this though, why start now if he's worried about the North West Turks and wants my help, unless he actually isn't really worried, doesn't want my help and is just testing me. Fuck. Even more fucked up is the prospect this might have been The Greek, making it look like Tottenham Sam's crew so that I'll start a war with them and be vulnerable. This shit's getting messy.

Jones.

MONDAY, 1st DECEMBER 1986
2030 HOURS
MY SECERET HOUSE, CORNER OF SECOND AVENUE AND ESPANADE, FRINTON-ON-SEA

Fuck me, what a week. Got to get out of the madness and lay low for a few days. Had a right ball-ache getting up here too. Drove to Braintree, parked up on a back-street not far from the station, then got a train to Colchester, then, jumped in a taxi, getting the dickhead driver to drop me at the centre of town, walking the remainder of the journey. Can't be too careful though, can't afford to be followed. Need a shit, food too, I'm fucking starving.

Jones.

MONDAY, 1st DECEMBER 1986
2105 HOURS
MY SECERET HOUSE, CORNER OF SECOND AVENUE AND ESPANADE, FRINTON-ON-SEA

Great shit, managed to knock one out too, relieve some tension. Anyhow, it was defo Sam's crew who rumbled the Star Lane shop, a friend of Dex reckons he heard Sam and a few others boasting about it at a blues party at The Farm. With that, plus the shooting of Bee, we're battling on all fronts, if I'm honest, feels like everything is getting out of control. Thinking of Bee, he's out of hospital now, currently laid up at his old-dears house, bless her. She adopted him when he was just a baby and he's been a little shit ever since. Friday night, Me, Will and a few of the hardcore get tooled up and head down to Cheeks nightclub in the arse end of nowhere, (Deptford to me and you), to have it large with the door-crew, The Greeks guys. Tiny's usually on the door but is nowhere to be seen so we steam in, smashing the fuck out of the five or six guys on the door before running through the club causing havoc. Smashing every bottle in the place, we rob the till and chin the Manager, the clueless prick. Straight after, we head to one of The Greeks shops on a stinking estate behind Lewisham train station. Bolt-cutter through the outer gate, we kick the door in and the two little muggy cunts inside get smashed up. We take the stock, a couple of ounces of coke and some weed, plus a couple of grand in cash. Hold up, fucking foods arrived. Blimey, that's quick.

Jones.

TUESDAY, 2nd DECEMBER 1986
0837 HOURS
MY SECERET HOUSE, CORNER OF SECOND AVENUE AND ESPANADE, FRINTON-ON-SEA

Had a pizza then flaked out, slept straight through. To be honest, haven't slept like that for as long as I can remember. Last Saturday I got busy on the blower ringing around each of my shops, got twelve of them now, checking everything's okay and telling them to get extra security in, a few more spotters around the way too, maybe even arm up if they haven't already. Then, I get a random call, says it's Sam. Well, fuck me sideways. Screaming down the phone, he's yelling he knows it was me who robbed his gaff on The Farm, that I'm a dead-man walking and all that blah-blah-blah bullshit. Listen you cunt and listen good, I say. You fucking robbed me, not the other way around, I don't need no fucking yardie-crack bollocks on my hands, all I want is my stock back, my cash back and whoever smashed up my lad dealt with. Oi, he says, slow and low. You would say that, wouldn't you, you fucking "dutty-egit-fool", (his words). Have it your way, he whispers, this is fucking war. Phone goes dead and I'm left looking at the receiver. I have literally no fucking idea of what he's going on about, we didn't rob any of his places.

Jones.

WEDNESDAY, 3rd DECEMBER 1986
1413 HOURS
MY SECERET HOUSE, CORNER OF SECOND AVENUE AND ESPANADE, FRINTON-ON-SEA

Ahh, just back from a nice walk along the seafront. I fucking love the sea, gives me time to think. I've been in constant contact with the shops, they're okay right now, there's been no repeat of the Star Lane robbery. I've been on top of Rude-Boy-Dee too, yeah, he's due to deliver 10-kee's on Friday. Fuck me, that's serious cash and serious time too if anyone gets caught. He's told me we all need to calm the fuck down before someone gets caught, or worse, killed. Says he's told Sam and The Greek the same. I know I should alert Hughes, but, fuck him, the cunt, he'll get all pussy about it and fuck things up. Dee's asked to do the trade at Southwold, something like 40 miles north of Harwich, he's paranoid about coming to London. I'm cool though, but, any further and I might as well go to Holland myself, which, come to think of it, is a thought. Anyhow, Southwold isn't far from Norwich, so might make a day of it and go see Kenny, if I can get a VO in time. Later on, I'll journey back to Braintree, get my motor, go meet Dee, see Kenny then head back to London and try and get this shit sorted out. Man, it never stops.

Jones.

FRIDAY, 5th DECEMBER 1986
1730 HOURS
FRONT SEAT OF MY CAR, OUTSIDE HMP NORWICH

Fuck me, just out from seeing Kenny, he's in a bad way. Piled on loads of weight, he's still rabbiting on about the two "gays", (as he put it), who did for him back in '81. Says he's studying now, reckons he'll have a degree by the time he gets out in a couple of years. Anyhow, met Rude-Boy-Dee earlier, had a good natter where he repeated his advice about finding a way to calm this shit down. Testing him out, I ask how Valentine's taking all this. Rolling his eyes, says he's got other shit going on right now having been arrested and charged with some shitty fencing charge, handling stollen money or something. Interesting, I'll pass this on to Hughes who will be able to cross-reference with any live cases, maybe we'll get to identify this clown.

Jones.

SATURDAY, 6th DECEMBER 1986
2200 HOURS
HOTEL VICTORIA, GROVE ROAD, HACKNEY

My flat in in Stepney's been fucked over, the fucking dirty slags. Door wide open, the place is tipped upside down, everything's smashed up and the cash under the bath-panel is gone. Thank god I took most of my shit up to the new house, nearly all the cash, my shooter, some personal coke too. No doubt the work of Sam or The Greek, no way this was a random burglary. Can't sleep there tonight, can't go to Bee's or Will's or Dex's for that matter for fear of being followed, so, I'm here in this piss-ridden, flea-bitten shithole, with the DSS dossers, rent boys and the fucking destitute. Thought about driving back to my secret gaff over in Frinton but it's miles away plus I've got shit to sort out first thing tomorrow so need to stay local. Interesting, telling Kenny about the shit with Sam and The Greek, he reckons I should play them both, let them both kill the shit out of each other while I hang around waiting to pick-up the pieces. Yeah, I like it, but, what the fuck would Hughes say when I report back that I've taken over South and North London, other than shitting his Liverpudlian pants, he'll probably call me back-in, withdraw me from the scheme, maybe even charge me, the fucking cocksucker. Let's face it, we both know, I aint ever going back, nah, how can I go back to being a full time proper policeman. Maybe I'll bribe him, get him on the payroll, yeah, that's why he's being a dick about everything, quoting the fucking PACE regs. I reckon he wants a piece of the action, yeah, fuck me, fucking cracked it Andy lad.

Jones.

MONDAY, 8th DECEMBER 1986
1320 HOURS
HOTEL VICTORIA, GROVE ROAD, HACKNEY

Mad busy yesterday, today too, haven't even been training. Called the number I had for Sam, he's still adamant he didn't do my place over. Yeah-yeah-yeah, I tell him we got to sort this shit out, otherwise someone will end up doing major-league time. Says no matter what, he knows for sure it was my lot who did his place on The Farm, so whoever did my place at Star Lane, actually did him a favour. Goes on to say in his eyes we've both been fucked over so we're about equal. Nah, olive branch or not, I tell him it's not equal, it'll never be equal, I don't fucking do equal, (these types would expect me to say shit like that). I've been fucked twice, but done fuck all to him. Even so, he's adamant he didn't do Star Lane, suggests maybe it was The Greek, he knows we've had issues over the young-lad who got killed, then the Blackheath bonfire and the Southend nightclub shooting. To be fair, I'm impressed, he's well informed. Okay, I say, suppose it was The Greek, I'll sort him out, but he needs to get a grip on The Farm. Maybe, as he first suspected, it's actually the Turks who robbed him. With a big sigh, he agrees it's his problem to sort. He sounds weary, like he's tiered and fucked off, much like me. We end with me telling him any more aggro, and it's all-out full-on blood in the streets war. He completely agrees. Good, we both know where we stand now, which is fine by me.

Jones.

MONDAY, 8th DECEMBER 1986
2300 HOURS
HOTEL VICTORIA, GROVE ROAD, HACKNEY

Chatting with Rude-Boy-Dee earlier, I tell him where I got to with Sam. Reckons we should just suck it all up and put it all down to experience, much better than all-out Los-Angeles gang warfare with total carnage, people doing serious time and money not being made. You know what, for a young guy, he's fucking cute. Says he's pretty much told The Greek the same, but he's too pig-headed to listen, says he's in a bad way over the Blackheath thing and wants me to hand Bee over. Fuck off, even if I could, no chance, he's like a brother. I've updated Hughes, given him what I know about the young lad who got killed, the Southend shooting and the scant details about Valentine. Like a pig in shit, says this is good info and will keep the higher-uppers at bay for a while. The souse twat.

Jones.

SUNDAY, 4th JANUARY 1987
0835 HOURS
MY FLAT, GLOBE ROAD, STEPNEY

Fuck-fuck-fuck-fuck. Dex is dead.
Fuck.

SUNDAY, 4th JANUARY 1987
0850 HOURS
MY FLAT, GLOBE ROAD, STEPNEY

Can't believe I've written those words. Shot, outside a pub in New Cross, gunshot to the chest. Can't believe it. Dex, I'm so sorry.

SUNDAY, 4th JANUARY 1987
0920 HOURS
MY FLAT, GLOBE ROAD, STEPNEY

Can't stop crying, I never cry. Had Sue on the phone earlier, crying her eyes out too, she's still at Guys Hospital. Just got off the phone to the fucking Greek cunt, got him out of bed by the sound of it, the lazy fat fuck. New Cross is his manor, his back yard, his responsibility. Sounded genuinely shocked, says he knows jack shit, but will ask around pronto. He fucking better do, or he's dead. I'll go see Bee and Will in a bit, get this sorted. I can't believe it. Poor Sue. This shit's got to end.

Jones.

MONDAY, 5th JANUARY 1987
1800 HOURS
MY FLAT, GLOBE ROAD, STEPNEY

Headed down to New Cross yesterday, not entirely sure why, just driving around, popping in and out of a few pubs, asking some questions. Nothing though, zero, zilch. The Greek came back too, says he's heard nothing, that whoever did it wasn't on his team, but, the pub in question, The Woodpecker, is a sleazy shithole frequented by low-life. Says he usually sets up shop there, but it got raided a week or so ago so hasn't bothered since. Sounds fucking fishy to me, I don't believe him. He goes on to say the madness has to stop, fighting between ourselves is crazy and doing none of us any favours. Says the tit for tat between our firms is about even, Bee got what he deserved so we should leave it there. He's promised to help me find out who did for Dex. Too right, that's the important thing, so for now, a cease-fire makes sense. Sue and the kids are at her mums now. The funeral's planned for 3 weeks time, pending the Coroner releasing him. I've told her I'll sort all that out for her. Fuck, still can't believe it. Why Dex, why?

Andrew Jones.

TUESDAY, 5th JANUARY 1987
2200 HOURS
MY FLAT, GLOBE ROAD, STEPNEY

Met with Hughes today, face to face at a greasy spoon near Upminster train station. Professional, over-pronouncing every word, felt like our conversation was being recorded for future evidence, yeah, he can fuck right off though, I'm not being played like a pussy, the cunt. I'm defo not offering him part of the business neither, not a single penny. Reciting some of the PACE regs and Code of Conduct shit, says, with the recent violence and now a close associate being killed, I'm being formally withdrawn from the COG10 programme, for my own good. Own good, fuck off. He goes on to say the higher-uppers want me to introduce a new colleague into the "theatre" (his word), who'll eventually take over from me. Nah-nah-nah, no fucking way I'm doing that, these villains will see it a mile off and I'll be topped, they're fucking idiots for sure, but not stupid. I need to know what my options are, how can I play this to my advantage. Maybe I'll go over his head to the higher-uppers, tell them it'll be a mistake to withdraw me, maybe go see John, haven't seen him in ages come to think of it. He's way too detached now though, too corporate, too much of a brown-bread-munching-follow-the-rules-shine-your-shoes pleb. China, that's who I need, blast from the past, he's been around the block, he knows the score, he's on the edge of dodgy, yeah, let's see what he thinks.

Jones.

FRIDAY, 6th FEBRUARY 1987
1750 HOURS
MY FLAT, GLOBE ROAD, STEPNEY

Took ages to track China down. Turns out he's now attached to the Murder Squad, (the Major Incident Group, as it's officially known), seconded as "Special Advisor" to the Sussex Police, investigating the murder of two little girls. Sounds fucking awful, despicable, soul destroying. Says he's heard about COG10 and the deep undercover work, then congratulates me for being the longest serving deep-cover officer. Interesting, I never knew that. His advice is I should accept being withdrawn, it's for the right reasons and I'm sure to be looked after when I'm back in. Goes on to say, the other option is to go completely rogue, fuck Hughes and fuck the Met, just do my own thing for a few years then retire to Spain. Reckons unless I commit murder, chances are they'll never charge me for fear of being seen to have propped up the cocaine business for a couple of years, the exact same years when consumption and drug related violence has exploded. He's smart, I never really thought about it that way. Says if they carry on paying me every month, it's absolute proof beyond any reasonable doubt I'm still a copper. Very true my friend, he's a genius. He goes on to say, if I do go rogue, then I'll need friends in the know, friends who can keep an eye out, tipping me the wink at the right time. Yeah, I get it, but, who could possibly be up for that, I wonder. Laughing, says everyone would be up for it, assuming the price is right. Bingo, he's in and on the payroll.

Jones.

SATURDAY, 14th FEBRUARY 1987
2210 HOURS
MY FLAT, GLOBE ROAD, STEPNEY

Just heading out, going to stop off at Southend to see Bee who's back on the doors, then over to Frinton to chill the fuck out. Might also go see Kenny before heading back here in a few days. Heard back from The Greek the other day, reckons he's found the guy who did Dex, a no-mark teenager holding a shooter for his uncle or something. The idiot gets pissed-up and starts larging it around the pub, billy-big-balls threatening everyone and being a prick. Dex, mister wrong-place-at-the-wrong time, gets blasted after a short confrontation. The Greek says he's no idea why he was deep south, or in that particular shit-hole, but will keep asking questions. Says he'll pick the little shit up whenever we're ready, and, until then, he'll keep an eye on him in case he tries to do one. We'll get the funeral out of the way, then deal with the little cunt.

Jones.

FRIDAY, 20th FEBRUARY 1987
1722 HOURS
MY FLAT, GLOBE ROAD, STEPNEY

Just got back from a few days away. I love Frinton, it's a piece of me, soon as I'm done with this madness I'm retiring down there, the steady life and all that. Saw Kenny earlier, yeah, looks a bit more chipper, reckons he might get out on early release within a year. Personally, I doubt it, maybe a couple of years, but not yet. Telling him about what happened to Dex was one of the hardest things I've had to do, didn't take it well at all, welled up in fact. In our teens, we all hung out together so he knew Dex just as much as I did. He made me promise, indeed swear we'll sort it out, eye for an eye style. That, my friend, I can most certainly promise.

Jones.

SATURDAY, 21st FEBRUARY 1987
0210 HOURS
MY FLAT, GLOBE ROAD, STEPNEY

Dex's funeral yesterday, fuck me, cried my eyes out, I've known him since primary school, St Lukes at Canning Town. His mum and my mum used to go shopping together on Saturday mornings, down to the market on the High Road. Can't believe he's actually gone, I'm half expecting him to walk through the door any time. A decent send-off though, all the ICB attended, of course, plus a load of other season ticket holders who sit near us, even a few retired players, Ant Bedley and Willy Gilts. We also had a few other minor celebrities such as Dave Ford, the world darts champion, Benji Stephens, the aspiring world boxing champ and Loraine Aspreni, the former page 3 stunner, (who's still got it by the way). To be honest, I was surprised how many people actually attended, didn't really appreciate how well connected he was. I told Sue I'll take care of the costs, but to be honest, Bee had already paid it all up, including the wake. I gave Sue's old dear an envelope with £100k in to tide them over for a bit while they sort out his estate. The funeral's at Walthamstow cemetery, and the wake at Woodford Golf Club, he was a member there apparently, fuck, I didn't even know he played golf. Still can't believe he's gone. Just doesn't feel right not having him around, he's my mate, my best mate I suppose. Fuck it, I'm actually completely lonely, I don't really belong anywhere. Fuck me, it's the fucking beer talking, making me sound like a pleb. Later today we're off to set things right, avenge our friend and brother, yeah, we're off deep-south.

Jones.

SUNDAY, 22nd FEBRUARY 1987
1435 HOURS
MY FLAT, GLOBE ROAD, STEPNEY

Headed to the Limelight on Shaftsbury Avenue early evening, made sure we're clocked on the security cameras and by as many faces as possible. Then, we do a quick one out the back, then down the fire escape, being picked up by one of Bee's men in a robbed Cortina with dodgy plates. Forty minutes later we're down at New Cross Gate tube station, where we meet Tiny who squeezes in the back. Directing us through a fuck-awful estate to the Woodpecker Pub, he tells us to hold tight before disappearing inside. Five minutes later he comes out dragging a scrawny piece of dogshit, a skinny teenage retch with a wedge haircut and fuck-awful acne. Chucking him into the boot, we hear the little shit bawling, before crying and eventually sobbing. Fuck him. Driving slowly through the estate we stop at a kids slide and round-a-bout, opposite one of the tower-blocks. Dragging the little cunt out by his hair, we kick the living shit out of him with Bee stamping on his head. Will and Tiny drag his unconscious body into the lift lobby, and, a few minutes later, he's launched off the top. I fucking heaved at the sight of it, but, zero emotion, a life for a life yeah. Tiny gives us all a hug, tells us he's sorry about Dex then jogs off into the dark night. Making our way back to the Limelight in total silence, we head back through the fire escape and have a quiet drink, toasting our friend. Got back here about 0100-hours. Thought about calling Clare, just to have someone close, but, fuck it, what's done is done.

Jones.

MONDAY, 23rd FEBRUARY 1987
0710 HOURS
MY FLAT, GLOBE ROAD, STEPNEY

Woke up a lot last night, an awful night to be fair, kept thinking about the scrawny young lad. Although he fucking deserved everything he got, the cunt, he killed Dex, I keep thinking about the terror he must have felt, and the sorrow his parents must feel, just like Sue and the kids. Two families, ruined. Even though an eye for an eye is the way, it doesn't take away the pain. I miss Dex, always will.

Andrew Jones.

THURSDAY 9th APRIL 1987
1200 HOURS
MY FLAT, GLOBE ROAD, STEPNEY

Went down to West Ham last night, short notice thing with Bee calling at 1700-hours asking if I'm free. We won 3-one against the Arsenal, no trouble though, fine by me to be honest. Will hasn't been to the football all season apparently, been busy setting up a pirate radio station, so Bee's says anyway. Fuck me, he's way too old for all that palaver. Felt subdued last night, pretty shit to be honest, the season has gone to shit, we're just above the relegation zone having won only twice in the last 10 games. Neither Will nor Bee have mentioned what happened down in New Cross, which suits me fine truth be told. I've been working hard to get more product in, tough going actually as the police, boarder officials and the coastguard are on high alert. Dee tells me the last shipment came in via Aberdeen in Scotland, then couriered down here in a series of cars. Me and The Greek have been on better terms since the New Cross thing, he's even invited me down to a new club night one of his pals is opening on the Brighton seafront. Might well go down, see what it's all about, build some bridges too. Off to the gym now, then, later on, I'm on my collections round. We've got 13 shops now, each of them doing good business with heavily cut coke, speed and cannabis resin too.

Jones.

THURSDAY, 16th APRIL 1987
1915 HOURS
MY FLAT, GLOBE ROAD, STEPNEY

Heading to Brighton in a bit, just waiting for Sammie to arrive then we're off. Oh yeah, new bird yeah, Sammie. Fuck me, she's fit as fuck, tall, blonde, super fit body, plus, she loves cock, fucks hard on coke too. Reckon it'll take me a couple of hours to get down to the south coast, which is okay, The Greek says it doesn't get lively till midnight anyway. That's late, especially on a weekday too, I'll have to do a few lines I reckon, (any excuse).

Jones.

FRIDAY, 17th APRIL 1987
1430 HOURS
MY FLAT, GLOBE ROAD, STEPNEY

So, I've seen to the future. The club night The Greek took me to is less of a night "club", more a black hole of music. Practically pitch-black, no lights or furniture or anything really, just a space beneath some railway arches, with the loudest speakers I've ever heard playing, so The Greek says, Chicago warehouse music, sounds like disco if you ask me. Out back of the arches, me and him share a few joints and chat about old times, Dex too for that matter. Then, bolt out of the blue, he asks if I'm still a copper. What the fuck? Says he's knocking off a bird who works in the Tax Office, who's looked me up. What the fuck? Says I'm paying income tax and receiving regular payments from the Metropolitan Police. Fucking hell. Thinking quickly, I tell him part of my exit package included several years salary payments and pension contributions, otherwise, I'd kick up a storm and get the unions involved. Slitty eyes, he's not sure if I'm talking bollocks, says he's always been impressed I've never been lifted, or done any time. Just fucking smart, aren't I, I say with a wink, acknowledging a slither of truth. Listen, I tell him, once a copper, always a copper, nobody ever really leaves the police. Yeah, I understand, he smiles, passing me the joint. Too fucking right you do, you clueless cunt.

Jones.

TUESDAY, 5th MAY 1987
1530 HOURS
MY FLAT, GLOBE ROAD, STEPNEY

Got back from the gym a while ago, had a shower, a wank and a bit of a kip, and now, after a few lines, I'm wide awake ready to go. Yesterday, fuck me, things got wild. Got a call from The Greek early doors, asked if I wanted to go to a dog fight with him. Yeah, okay, fuck it, I say, never been to one before. Picking me up, we head into Kent, ending up at a disgusting pig farm, way past Maidstone. Parking up, it's busy with sheds and barns all over, plus loads of fucking gypsies yelling and balling everywhere. In one shed there's a bare-knuckle fight going on, blood and cash everywhere (travellers love fighting and betting in equal measure), while in another, there's first a cock-fight, which isn't for me, nah, then dogs, two American Pitbulls. Both the birds and the dogs fight to the death, and it takes fucking ages for them to kill each other. It's gut wrenching if I'm honest, disgusting, not my scene at all, nah, give me the bare-knuckle shit all day long. The Greek seems pre-occupied by a nasty looking piece of work handling bundles of cash being bet on various dogs. "Bobby Love", he nudges, not to be fucked with. Rumour is, he smiles, he's Rude-Boy-Dee's boss… Hang-a-fucking-bout, Bobby Love, from the fucking Heathrow gold-bullion job, is actually "Valentine", mister-big of the London cocaine industry, and, he's Dee's boss? Fuck right off. He stares at me, eyebrows arched, not knowing my inner dialogue is in complete turmoil. Fuck me, Bobby Love is Valentine, fucking-hell, "love" equals "valentine", I can't believe it. This is gold dust, kryptonite, fucking diamond encrusted turbo-crack, I can hear Hughes' balls exploding from the other side of London.

Jones.

SATURDAY, 11th JULY 1987
2300 HOURS
MY FLAT, GLOBE ROAD, STEPNEY

Soppy bollocks, fucking hell. Just here to grab a bag. Last night I'm out with Sammie for some drinks, stayed local over here at Bethnal Green. Several lines and multiple drinks later, she fancies a kebab, so we head down to Heart of Istanbul. Minding our own business, wrapping her arms around me, she's grinding onto my baseball bat of a cock when a bunch of pissed up dickheads walk in. I hear one of them whispering to his mate about how "the big fucker", (i.e. me), could pull a stunner like her, (i.e. her). Well, a what-did-you-say-smash-bang-wallop later, one of the cunts is put through the plate glass window, one runs off like a pussy while the other one stands firm, gobbing off, giving it the big-un. Horny as fuck, I'm now well and truly fucked off too, so, reaching over the counter, I grab the two-foot long carving knife. Fuck me if the mugs arm practically comes clean off, blood everywhere, attempted murder, no fucking doubt. Had it away lively, got to get the fuck out of London, out of England maybe. Cash plus some pants in a bag, Sammie's off home in a taxi while I'm off to Frinton then fuck knows where.

Jones.

TUESDAY, 14th JULY 1987
1330 HOURS
MY SECERET HOUSE, CORNER OF SECOND
AVENUE AND ESPANADE, FRINTON-ON-SEA

Just off the blower to Hughes, haven't spoken to him in ages. Says enough is enough, there's too much violence, too many drugs, too little arrests, plus rumours of various other serious offenses and now, attempted murder. He's instructed me to hand myself in, I'm officially no longer a COG10 operative, my Letter of Authority has been revoked. Phone down, fuck off cunt, fucking hate that guy, and to think, I was once in awe of him. Then, I speak with China, he's heard about what happened on Saturday at the kebab shop, says I should do one out of the country. We still don't have a treaty with Spain apparently, so I could go "all Marbella" and just disappear. He's right, I could, but, I'll always have this hanging over me and, all things being equal, I could never come home. Or, he says, I could try to bargain with Hughes and take a nominal charge for Common Assault. Fucking hell, I never thought it would end this way. Next up, I call Arry, who starts swearing at me in Jewish or Yiddish or whatever, says he can protect my assets by transferring them to a trust, or something, but says I should try to convert as much as possible to physical cash, and lock it away in a safe deposit box. Good advice.

Fucked as a 50-year old whore, Jones.

THURSDAY, 16th JULY 1987
1700 HOURS
MY SECERET HOUSE, CORNER OF SECOND
AVENUE AND ESPANADE, FRINTON-ON-SEA

So, it's all set. Hughes will take me in, I get a serious bollocking and officially removed from COG10, then redeployed into traffic or community or some other bullshit detail, all over a fucking pleb giving it large. I've asked Bee to assume control of the shops, he's fine with it all, will probably do a better job than me anyway. I've told Dee too, he's properly gutted, sounded upset, disappointed even. Says Valentine won't be happy with this level of attention, but, he'll manage him. Fuck knows when I'll next write, but, for now, I'd like to say it's been fun, but can't, reality is, it's been shit.

Jones.

WEDNESDAY, 31st AUGUST 1988
1315 HOURS
MUM AND DADS, RUSCOE ROAD, CANNING TOWN

Hello again, remember me? Yeah, I'm the under-cover-ex-copper turned underworld big-time-charlie who got locked the fuck up. Where to start? Went to hand myself in to the fucking snake, Hughes, the cunty mother-fucker, who immediately arrests me for attempted murder of the kebab-shop pleb, and conspiracy to import and supply a controlled substance, aka, wholesale drug dealing. After some horse-trading, union involvement and various threats to go public and production of my letter, I agree to the lesser charge of Grievous Bodily Harm Without Intent. Although this carries a maximum 5-year term, I'm given assurances my circumstances and the letter will mitigate this down to a non-custodial sentence. Few weeks later I'm on remand and a dickhead child-molesting judge gets a hard-on and I get 25-months, out in 13 for good behaviour. Even worse, I did most of the time up north in Leeds, in a fucking decrepit castle of a prison, not easy to keep my nose clean in there. My salary payments ceased straight away, which means I'm officially out, out for real, out proper. Fuck them and fuck Hughes, they can all fuck right off. I literally risked my life for them, only to be treated like this, makes me want to puke. As for Hughes, he's now on the retribution list, the fucking scouse cunt. I don't know how, or when, but that fat fuck has it coming.

Jones (is back, baby!)

THURSDAY, 1st SEPTEMBER 1988
1015 HOURS
MUM AND DADS, RUSCOE ROAD, CANNING TOWN

The old dear has me up at 0800-hours every day with a full English, bless her. Out and about yesterday, so much has changed. Arry sold my place in Stepney, I bought the whole block after Dex died, ended up making a decent turn on it. He managed to hide most of my other assets, yeah, the "supply of drugs" charges didn't stick so there's no grounds for any asset recovery, thank fuck. Bee's sorted the business, along with Rude-Boy-Dee, in fact, they've grown it massively, diversifying into ecstasy pills. These babies sound the bollocks, I fully intend trying some later tonight. Bee's in complete control now, clearly more cut out for it than I ever was. Think I'll offer him the business full time, it's basically debt collecting and putting dickheads in line. Reckon I'll become the Chairman or something, yeah, he can pay me a modest royalty each week. Sounds pretty cool, although I don't need the cash, Arry tells me I have a "book value" of £3m plus about £600k in cash in the safe at Frinton, so, we're sitting pretty.

Chairman Jones, (yeah, I like that, a lot.)

FRIDAY, 2nd SEPTEMBER 1988
0835 HOURS
MUM AND DADS, RUSCOE ROAD, CANNING TOWN

Turns out Bee's throwing me a "welcome home" party in a warehouse in Stratford. I appreciate the sentiment, but in a fucking warehouse? He's lined up the whole crew plus The Greek, which will be nice. I've called up Sammie, but her number just rings out now, no doubt she's moved on with her life. Shit me, I even thought about Claire, but, just can't do it. Locked up inside gives you nothing but time to think, time to put things into perspective. Not to worry, I'll find a bit of skirt down there tonight I reckon, yeah, neck a few beers and bingo, we're in.

Jones.

SUNDAY, 4th SEPTEMBER 1988
1655 HOURS
MUM AND DADS, RUSCOE ROAD, CANNING TOWN

Fuck me, feel just about normal now. The come-downs from ecstasy are a fucking nightmare, how these kids do it week in week out, I'll never know, but, fucking hell, the buzz is totally worth it. Energy, confidence, euphoria, just like coke, (I do love coke), but also a sense of love, warmth, togetherness, I don't fucking know how to explain it. Oh, and the dancing, I never dance, not in my nature, but, an hour in with the music, (oh, the music), the lazers and the lights, mate, I'm on it, moving and grooving, bobbing and weaving. I actually lost Bee and the others for most of the night, found them again when the sun was coming up. Saw Will there too, he's got a load of kids deejaying for him now at these raves and his pirate radio station. He's on ecstasy too, loving it, loving me, rabbiting on about the old times. I like him, I'm gutted about what happened between him and Bee, but, that's life I suppose. The Greek was there too, hugging me, telling me he's missed our banter, we ought to work together again soon, maybe get together and sort that cunt Sam out. I know he was testing me, seeing if prison has changed me, but yeah, the more I think about it, I do owe Sam, just for old times sake.

Jones.

SUNDAY, 25th SEPTEMBER 1988
2355 HOURS
KENNY'S OLD PLACE, LAUDERDALE
HEIGHTS, THE BARBICAN, LONDON

What a touch. Been staying with the folks since getting out, but I can't stay there long-term, nah, it's not right a six-foot-six, 18-stone guy touching 30-years old stays with his parents, nah. Called Kenny last week for a chat, he gets 10 minutes phone-time a week as part payment for working in the canteen. Says he's still got his place at the Barbican, the one he bought outright just before getting locked up in '81. Reckons his old man told him he's being chased for 11-grands worth of service charge, so, if I clear this for him I can stay there till he gets out. Bingo. Moved in last Wednesday, took a day to clean it out, it fucking stunk, the dirty pig. The furniture needs updating, and the décor looks like a slags puked up on the walls, but, it's pretty cool around here, all professional city-boy types and fit secretaries with short skirts. Been out each weekend since getting out, warehouses seem to be the "in-thing" now, nightclubs aren't cool any more. Still, been dropping ecstasy which is great, along with a few lines of coke as a livener, yeah, just the ticket. The come-downs, especially not being able to sleep is a shitter though, can't help being pulled into a downer, dwelling on the past thinking about Dex and Claire and that young lad in New Cross, even Janice for fucks sake. Look lively Jonesy-lad, sort yourself out son.

Jones.

SUNDAY, 25th SEPTEMBER 1988
MIDNIGHT
KENNY'S OLD PLACE, LAUDERDALE
HEIGHTS, THE BARBICAN, LONDON

Sorry about this, it comes on in waves sometimes, just a surge of feeling down, dark, basically like shit. I know I sound like a pansy or a fucking pleb, but I can't help dwelling on the gutter-scum inside, the horrors I saw and heard. Grown men, big guys, strong as an ox-types crying and weeping, wanking themselves into oblivion or bumming the weaker guys who'd scream out for their mums. I don't think it's sex, nah, they need to feel powerful, in control, turns my fucking stomach, the dirty cunts. You know, while in Leeds, two fellas killed themselves, one hung himself in his cell with his bedsheet, the other cut is own throat, yeah, actually slit his own throat while in the showers. Fuck me, I'll never forget seeing the limp, literally white corpse surrounded by more blood than you'd think was possible. Fucking hell, I'm a million miles from the young guy who made his mum and dad proud when passing out at Hendon. I remember them helping me with my spelling on my application form, then the smiles when they opened the letter inviting me for the tests. I miss that guy. Fuck, the downers.

Jones.

SATURDAY, 8th OCTBER 1988
1040 HOURS
MY SECERET HOUSE, CORNER OF SECOND AVENUE AND ESPANADE, FRINTON-ON-SEA

Had to get away. Me, Bee and The Greek agreed to turn over Sam's factory, where he turns coke into crack, located out the back of a taxi-shop next to Bruce's Grove train station, maybe half-a-mile from The Farm. He'll defo know it's us, so, I've told Bee to close the shops for the weekend, let the punters cluck while I come down here to lay-low. Instead of meeting The Greek as planned, Tiny turns up in his tidy RS Cosworth, along with 2 hard as nails looking ugly mugs. Says The Greek's been arrested earlier in the day for no car insurance or something, says we should go ahead as planned as he's got it on good authority Sam was due a big delivery today. Fine by me, the prick gets fucked up either way. Forty minutes later, we pull up a hundred meters down the road in a small residential street with decent houses either side. Climbing out, we shimmy along in the shadows till we're outside what looks to be a shitty wooden back door. Tiny tells his two guys to wait outside and I tell Bee the same. Pistol out of the back of his trousers, Tiny slams into the door and the entire frame and a portion of wall comes away. In a flash he's in and I follow. Inside, it's mayhem, utter carnage. two guys shot, (by Tiny), one guy floored by me and two skinny-retch women laid out unconscious courtesy of Tiny. Back in the car, we have what looks like a kilo or so of coke, a bag-bag of maybe 500-rocks of crack and about 4-grand in cash, plus a tasty sawn-off I'll be keeping.

Jones.

WEDNESDAY, 12th OCTBER 1988
1040 HOURS
KENNY'S OLD PLACE, LAUDERDALE HEIGHTS, THE BARBICAN, LONDON

Just back from a meet with The Greek, turns out he wasn't actually arrested the other day when we turned over Sam's place, nah, says he got pulled over and feared he was being followed so laid low. Total bullshit. We met on Tower Bridge, right in the middle, half-way between our empires, importantly, in plain sight of the public and no end of witnesses. Sam has declared nuclear war on us both, he can't be seen to take this from anyone, so we need to sort something out. Turns out, The Greek's play is to sit it out as a neutral, washing his hands of the robbery then come in after the event as peace-keeper, the fucking mug. Says he's squared it all with Sam, says Sam will leave it be as long as a) Tiny hands over one of his men, blaming him for going rogue and b) The Greek confirms I'm out, retired from the business and Bee has taken over for good. Pretty smart move to be fair, says this way, we get revenge on Sam, I get an "out" while he gets leverage over Sam. Seems to make sense, perfect sense actually, yeah he's smart. Says Rude-Boy-Dee is cool with the arrangement too, just wants everyone to calm the fuck down as Valentine and the crew in Europe are spooked by the violence, and the sudden shift to ecstasy. I'm relieved in a weird way, but sad too, booted out of the Met, done my time inside and now, in effect, sacked from my own drug empire. What a life.

Jones.

THURSDAY, 13th OCTBER 1988
2247 HOURS
KENNY'S OLD PLACE, LAUDERDALE
HEIGHTS, THE BARBICAN, LONDON

Just back from bandit country, deep-south, fuck me it's grim around there. Tiny has a flat in the middle of a shithole estate not far from Deptford market. I don't usually head down that way, certainly not on my own, but I need some powder and I don't fancy going to see Bee cap in hand, nah, fuck that. Listen, I love ecstasy, it's the business, but, I'm also partial to a line or two, (or three), of coke to see me through. Walking in, he's on his weight bench pumping iron, yeah, he's nearly as big as me now. Over in the corner an older, skinny guy's sitting there smoking weed. An old friend apparently, according to Tiny he lived around Brixton at the time of the riots but nowadays is a nervous wreck. For a laugh, being sadistic pricks, we agree to wind him up a bit, shit the life out of him. I give him the big-un, the "don't I know you from somewhere" routine and see his face drop, he's petrified, scared, not knowing where to look, fun times. If Tiny wasn't such a prick, or a staunch Millwall man, I reckon we could have been mates although I was sure to remind him of our away fixture down at their shit-hole in December, yeah, his crew will be taught a proper lesson. He just smiled his big ugly smile, the fucking mug.

Jones.

FRIDAY, 14th OCTBER 1988
2110 HOURS
KENNY'S OLD PLACE, LAUDERDALE
HEIGHTS, THE BARBICAN, LONDON

Heading to the Astoria on Tottenham Court Road tonight. With a few of his deejays there, Will's been promoting it furiously on his pirate station, "Mid-Pressure Radio", (fuck knows why he called it that). There're a few other pirate stations, like Dream FM, which I like and a legal station, Lips FM, but that's way too poncy. They're all playing the same warehouse music, it's massive, everywhere I go I hear it all day every day, corner shops, market stalls, clubs, pubs, even kids walking down the street are signing these songs over and over. So, I met, yes, actually met with China today, haven't seen him in years. Fuck me, he looks old, I mean, I look old, weathered maybe, but I've put on maybe 3-stone in muscle, whereas he's got grey, fat too. He called me up when I stopped the regular payments to him a few weeks back, yeah, he had a right old moan. I told him I'm out, it's not my business no more, but will hook him up with Bee if he wants. For old times sake I'll toss him a few morsels of info just to wet his appetite, like, for example, The Greek is the ring-leader, working directly for Valentine. Yeah, that'll keep them all working overtime, hopefully get The Greek some unwanted attention too. We agree to keep in touch, but, feels like a goodbye to be honest, good riddance too, the fucking clown.

Jones.

MONDAY, 21st NOVEMBER 1988
2005 HOURS
KENNY'S OLD PLACE, LAUDERDALE HEIGHTS, THE BARBICAN, LONDON

Bored, bored, bored. I've still got my kosher businesses and investments to keep me busy including the betting shops, Dex's old car business I bought soon after he passed, and a couple of taxi-offices too, but, touring around these, checking they're running okay is a fucking bore. I've decided, for Christmas, I'll buy my mum and dad their own place, somewhere out of the city, nice, it's the least I can do. Arry says getting hold of a couple of hundred-grand in cash will raise suspicions, so suggests I win big on the horses, have a winter sale at the car-lot or sell a stake I have in "Real-Sec", a city firm who buy up brown-belt land in preparation for redevelopment. This will be more than enough for a nice house at Westcliffe-on-Sea, yeah, my old mum's dreamt about retiring out there. Out of the blue I get a call the other day from a probation officer at HMP Norwich, suggests they're planning a release date for Kenny, possibly in 3-months' time. Fuck me, that's quick, earlier than I expected. Apparently, he put me down as a future employer, saying I've agreed to give him a job. Of course, I tell the clueless prick, he'll be running my Executive Car Sales company, aka, Dex's old car lots. Everything seems in order and the probation guy sounds happy. Honestly, this is great news, I'm pleased for him, as long as he can keep his nose clean until then. Family is important.

Jones.

SATURDAY, 2nd DECEMBER 1988
2305 HOURS
KENNY'S OLD PLACE, LAUDERDALE HEIGHTS, THE BARBICAN, LONDON

Big day tomorrow, the day of all days, Millwall away. Still can't believe it, at last, we can have it off and see who has the top team. Bee and Will have been buzzing all week, I must have had a dozen calls from each of them asking if I'll be there, reminding me over and over how important it is. Yeah-yeah, I get it, this is it, the big one, I can't fucking wait. I've had The Greek on the blower too, bigging it up, having a laugh, telling me my time has come and all that crap. Well, we'll fucking see, wont we, the big lumbering fuck. The plan is we'll meet in small groups to avoid the police, with me meeting some of the younger kids at Canning Town. We'll then make our way to London Bridge station where we'll meet Will and his crew, then get an overground train to New Cross to meet Bee and his mob, who'll be getting the tube. Reckon we'll have at least 300-hardcore, and probably the same again of joiner-inner casuals. We plan to march army-style through New Cross to their shit-hole ground, then have it large. Bee says The Greek wouldn't commit to a formal meet, instead, warned us to be on our toes when we enter bandit country. We've got the return fixture at our ground in April, reckon that'll be my last game as a hooligan, yeah, I'm way too old and too fucking tiered for all that shit, plus, I actually love West Ham and want to support the team as a normal punter, go and just enjoy the match. Anyhow, early night tonight, ready for war tomorrow.

Jones.

MONDAY, 4th DECEMBER 1988
0955 HOURS
KENNY'S OLD PLACE, LAUDERDALE
HEIGHTS, THE BARBICAN, LONDON

Had a right old laugh on Saturday, ended up with a shiner and bruised nose though. Soon as we get to New Cross train station, we're pelted by stones and bottles. Turning right out of the station, we walk for maybe 20-minutes and see the top of the stadium in the distance reaching above the back to back slum terraced houses of South East London. Singing "bubbles" as loud as possible, Bee and Will skurry around yelling "nobody runs, nobody hides". Turning into Cold Blow Lane, near the old Primary School, we're met by a sea of angry, a wall of fuck you, and, in the middle, The Greek, side by side with Tiny. In front of them, a line of clueless police, no more than 20 strong. We charge, they charge, it's chaos. The houses either side get smashed to fuck, police sirens can be heard in the distance above the hum of violence, grunts and yells. Yeah, the noise of bedlam, haven't heard sounds like that since '81 and the riot in Brixton. Bee gets to Tiny and they're tearing into each other before being drowned by the tidal wave of hate. Scanning around for The Greek, he's nowhere to be seen, the slippery fuck. Spinning around, I'm smashed around the head by some type of cosh. Fighting my way towards where I last saw Bee, a fleet of police horses gallop over, thank fuck, and the crowd parts a little. I see Will covered up on the floor with Bee above him, guard up spinning 360. Millwall backing off, we re-group, battered to fuck to be fair. Yeah, we got a doing, but, on the pitch we won 1-nil, and, we have them dirty fucks over to our place in a few months where they'll get theirs.

Jones.

SATURDAY, 17th DECEMBER 1988
1940 HOURS
KENNY'S OLD PLACE, LAUDERDALE HEIGHTS, THE BARBICAN, LONDON

Best day ever. Gave my mum and dad their house today, an early Christmas present. When I say house, I actually mean pub, they're not ready for retiring just yet. We saw a few nice gaffs down at Southend, overlooking the sea, but they fell in love with an old pub on the High Street, overlooking Bell Wharf Beach. Yeah, it's perfect, got a bit of a bit of a buzz about the place yet it's calm and mellow, lovely actually, plus, the old man's always fancied himself as a landlord. On top of that, while they legally own the flat above, I own the business below, so can push cash through there if needs be. Giving her the keys, the old dear cries her eyes out, hugs me then the old-fella. Tears in his eyes, says he's proud of me. He's never done that, choked me up to be fair. Makes all this totally worthwhile.

Andy Jones.

SUNDAY, 1st JANUARY 1989
1445 HOURS
MY SECERET HOUSE, CORNER OF SECOND
AVENUE AND ESPANADE, FRINTON-ON-SEA

Came over here yesterday after another freezing cold outdoor party. They're pretty much every weekend now, yesterdays happened to be a big one at Leeside Road in an old warehouse just by a low railway bridge. A decent night all in all, plus, the sound system was banging. Bee was there with a few of his crew, all younger lads, all out to make a name for themselves hanging around with a "living legend", yeah, that's how he's referred to nowadays. I always feel sad on New Years day. Most people are positive, thinking about the future, making New Years resolutions and all that bollocks, but, for me, I look back in time, back to the old-school. Yeah, my life changed when Dex died, no doubt about it. The more fragile life is, the less you value it, well, that's how I feel anyway. For all the different chapters of my life, the wrongs I've committed and the wealth I've now amassed, what have I really got to show for it. Sure, I've made my mum and dad proud, but at what cost. All they really know is I had my arse kicked out of the Met and now I've bought them their own gaff, with dirty, blood splattered drug money. What a life.

Jones.

TUESDAY, 17th JANUARY 1989
1030 HOURS
KENNY'S OLD PLACE, LAUDERDALE HEIGHTS, THE BARBICAN, LONDON

Just got off the blower, Kenny is due for release on Friday 17th February. Can't quite believe it actually, he's done his time, served his penance and now he's out, free, coming home a changed man. Bad times though, I'll have to move out. Fuck.

Jones.

MONDAY, 20th FEBRUARY 1989
1305 HOURS
KENNY'S OLD PLACE, LAUDERDALE
HEIGHTS, THE BARBICAN, LONDON

Fuck me, headache from hell, hangover from the devils arsehole. Kenny's out, got out on Friday. Picking him up outside the prison gates at 1000-hours, we head straight back to London and The George at Silvertown for a drink up with the chaps, a pretty quiet affair with Bee, Will and a few others. I'd forgotten how close Ken and Will were as mates, yeah, I was always closer to Dex, Kenny to Will. So anyway, Friday rolls into Saturday and we end up at the Astoria on Charring Cross Road for a "acid house" night. Charlie plus pills, we get royally fucked up. Kenny, wow, he fucking loves it, especially ecstasy. Next up, we got to get him laid, then to the gym, the fat cunt.

Jones

WEDNESDAY, 22nd FEBRUARY 1989
2130 HOURS
KENNY'S OLD PLACE, LAUDERDALE
HEIGHTS, THE BARBICAN, LONDON

Have to move out, can't live like this. After 8-years inside, Kenny needs his privacy, I get it. We had a good gym session today, even though a lardy fat fuck, he can still hit like a tank, but, he's slow, lost his sharpness, lost his eye. We had a good chat though, about the future, and the past. I tell him all about the Met, about COG10 and the deep undercover operation. Not one bit surprised, says he's heard about guys embedded into football crews, so stands to reason someone like me might has been selected. He's on about getting as much cash as possible then doing the off's to Spain, set up afresh over there and go straight. I get it, I envy his clarity, but, fuck me, he's obsessed with the clueless fucks he reckons set him up and got him put away. Says he knows for sure one has been put away on a life sentence for his part in the Tottenham riots a few years back, one is a city-boy who he thinks lives in New York while the other is shacked up with the sister of one of the Millwall crew. Interesting, I'll check with The Greek and Tiny, see what they know.

Jones

MONDAY, 27th FEBRUARY 1989
1745 HOURS
RENTED FLAT, GARNET STREET,
OVERLOOKING SHADWELL BASIN DOCK

Signed a lease on a 12-month rental gaff, fully furnished, not too shabby. Comes with a parking space and a nice view of what used to be the dock where, ironically, Kenny's old man used to work years back. I've checked with The Greek who says Kenny's number one wanted man is indeed shacked up with a tidy bit of skirt named Shirley. Turns out this guy "Devon" and Shirley are in loved-up bliss living in Greenwich, while he runs one of the biggest acid-house pirate stations in London, Dream FM, a direct competitor to Wills station. Fucking hell, my life is full of twists and turns, double-backs and loop-arounds, like a plot from an east-end soap opera. He's tight with Tiny apparently, says they're old-school friends or gay-for-each-other, or something. The Greek says it'll be World War Three if I go anywhere near him, reckons we should let it go.

Jones.

TUESDAY, 28th FEBRUARY 1989
1245 HOURS
RENTED FLAT, GARNET STREET,
OVERLOOKING SHADWELL BASIN DOCK

Spoke directly with Tiny. Turns out I've met this this joker Devon before, when I visited his flat for some personal use powder a while back. Yeah, we scared the be-jesus out of the fucking idiot when I pretended to know all about him. He looked like a scared little kid to be honest, not no world-class acid-house-pirate-radio rave promoter. Anyhow, he's promoting a rave this weekend, with Tiny doing the doors, so I'll mosey on down there and take a gander. I wont take Kenny, nah, he'll immediately want heads on spikes, limbs on the floor and graves dug deep. No time for that right now, got to play it smart.

Jones.

SUNDAY, 5th MARCH 1989
2030 HOURS
RENTED FLAT, GARNET STREET,
OVERLOOKING SHADWELL BASIN DOCK

Interesting. Went to the rave organised by this Devon chap at an old industrial unit at Three Mills Lane, Stratford. The best thing about the night were the deejays, yeah, they're pretty good, plus the sound-system was loud as fuck. But, overall it was a bit amateurish I suppose, but they still managed to get a couple of thousand punters in. Tiny says they banked £30k through the door and he sold £10-grands worth of ecstasy. Yeah, I see his play, he doesn't give a shit about the music or punters, as long as they're buying his stock. To be fair, with huge amounts of cash floating about it does sound interesting. Talking with Tiny, he wants to put on more and more raves, says Devon is actually a genius at promotion and put this particular rave on in a matter of weeks. Introducing me once more to Devon, I congratulate him on the rave, and, just for a laugh, fuck knows why, ask him if he'll be interested in promoting a rave I'll back financially. Fuck me sideways, his eyes well up and his bottom lip literally quivers, the fucking stuttering I-don't-know-it's-not-for-me fairy.

Jones.

FRIDAY, 10th MARCH 1989
1725 HOURS
RENTED FLAT, GARNET STREET,
OVERLOOKING SHADWELL BASIN DOCK

Met Kenny at the gym today, yeah, he's sharpening up nicely. I introduced him to the guy who sorts me with a few needles now and again, gave Kenny some white powder to dab before bed, reckons it'll burn fat while he sleeps. I told him about the rave at the weekend and how much cash was floating about, although nothing about that Devon chap. Face lighting up, I literally see pound-signs twinkling in his eyes, says we should get tooled up and rob these fucking plebs pronto. Nah-nah-nah Ken, I tell him, 20 or 30 large aint going to touch the sides mate, besides, once we do one of them, they'll all arm up then, before we know it, we'll be fighting in the trenches. Nodding along, says Will told him about a young guy putting on huge raves in aircraft hangers in Kent, with maybe 10-thousand punters. Now, 10's big, at least £100k through the gate, possibly £200k if we push the tickets to £20, probably the same again if we punted the ecstasy too. Tongue hanging out, he's drooling at the prospect of all this tax-free cash. What if we went massive, truly historic, fucking "Woodstock" ambitious, now we're talking, this is interesting money, good money, start-afresh-in-Spain money. Yeah, his little chubby face morphs into a smile, well, as close to a smile as we're ever going to get from him. He's in.

Jones.

SUNDAY, 26th MARCH 1989
2045 HOURS
RENTED FLAT, GARNET STREET,
OVERLOOKING SHADWELL BASIN DOCK

Last few weeks have been hectic, yeah, working out every day, seeing Bee regularly, visiting Will and his radio station on the Nightingale Estate as well as attending various raves and generally raving my tits off. Call it market research, if you like. What's clear is the punters love the adventure of it all, from the planning during the week through to the magical mystery tour on the night, ringing random telephone numbers for directions, meeting up outside tube stations or motorway services. Fuck knows what they get out of it, but they seem to love it. I've been harassing Tiny every other day about his pansy pal Devon helping us with the rave, he's adamant though, says he's not for hire, well, we'll see about that. I've arranged to see him during the week for a touch of personal, and, when I do, I'll tell him all about Kenny and Devon and his gay-pals grassing on him way back in '81. I'll tell him he either helps us put on a rave or we'll slit his throat, kill his kid, rape his bird then kill her too. I'll chuck in a few other grotesque details to spice it up, just to scare him even more. If that doesn't work, I'll tell him I'm still on the job, yeah, he and The Greek have suspected as much for years anyway. I'll say with what I have on him, The Greek and the whole fucking Millwall-tribe, they'll all get sent down, their assets grabbed, their families fucked over and all that political shit. Yeah, that'll do it.

Jones

TUESDAY, 28th MARCH 1989
1809 HOURS
RENTED FLAT, GARNET STREET,
OVERLOOKING SHADWELL BASIN DOCK

Enterprising little shit, Kenny's been talking with Will who's interested in promoting the rave too. Says the guys on his radio station have been putting on reasonably sized raves most weekends in the car park of Stratford Shopping Centre, reckons a huge, out of town rave will be a massive money spinner. Even better, (or worse, depending on how you look at it), him and Kenny have sorted a fucking venue too, a farm way out of London in Essex. Got to get a grip on this before Kenny takes over and it goes to shit. If he gets nicked again, he'll breach his license and be straight back inside, not to mention what might happen to me. Mate, I don't need this, don't need to get in this deep, I've made my money, I can fuck off out of it if I really want to. Yeah, I've managed to survive this long on my own, don't need my dickhead cousin fucking things up with any vendetta from the past. Fuck it, life's too short.

Jones.

FRIDAY, 31st MARCH 1989
1732 HOURS
RENTED FLAT, GARNET STREET,
OVERLOOKING SHADWELL BASIN DOCK

Bingo, Tiny and his devious little shit-cunt friend Devon are in, of course they are, the fucking numskulls. I've told The Greek, he's cool, in fact, he's up for taking Devon out full stop, says he's always fancied his bird, Shirley, the big sister of one of his up and coming lads called Lacy. Tiny says Devon wants to meet up, talk things over, get it all straightened out. Yeah, I respect that to be fair. Meeting them tomorrow south-side, in Woolwich, I fucking hate Woolwich, it's a shit-hole. Reason I've agreed to it is, unbeknown to Tiny, Kenny will be waiting over the other side of the Thames in Canning Town. Yeah, he wants a face-off with the fucking snake Devon, look him in the eye and make sure he knows this is strictly business, and, any fucking around will result in him being buried 6-feet under. Kenny's all about the cash, wants to start afresh, says he's big plans for Spain, righting a wrong from the past will only serve to fuck things up. Yeah, I get it, makes sense. At last, some fucking sound logic from him rather than his paranoid emotional bullshit.

Jones.

SATURDAY, 1st APRIL 1989
1905 HOURS
RENTED FLAT, GARNET STREET,
OVERLOOKING SHADWELL BASIN DOCK

Popped back for a shower, off to another rave tonight, well, a "rave night" in a shithole nightclub on Canvey Island Will's promoting. Yeah, a few nightclubs are trying to get in on the rave bandwagon and it's all a bit embarrassing to be honest. Earlier today I met with Tiny and dickhead Devon, he's literally shaking with fear the fucking pussy. Putting it on him big time, I tell him he's a cunt for what he did to Kenny so fucking owes us big time. Afterwards, I march him over to the ferry, then across the Thames to where Kenny is. Kenny gives him a few whacks to show him who's boss, then, acting his arse off, tells him it's not personal, it's all about the money and all he wants a fresh start. They fuck off back south, the clowns, bewildered as fuck. Yeah, they'll promote the rave, make us a fair chunk of cash, then we'll fuck them both over, the mugs.

Jones.

MONDAY, 3rd APRIL 1989
2205 HOURS
RENTED FLAT, GARNET STREET,
OVERLOOKING SHADWELL BASIN DOCK

Had to have a word with Kenny today, he's getting more and more erratic. I heard him and Will tried to rob an ATM machine, crashing a stolen lorry into it, the fucking idiots, those bastards are concreted in with 2-metre long hard as fuck steel rods anchoring them in place. Told him to calm the fuck down, be more discrete, take more precautions otherwise, he's straight back inside. Says he's had an idea, we should allow Devon to promote the rave, be the front face of it, the poster-boy if you will, then, if it comes on top with either police or rival gangs, (as if), he can take the fall. To be fair, this is a decent plan. Says he's seriously considering killing him, burying him in the woods behind the venue, reckons it'll be chaos on the night, nobody will ever know, he'll just be registered as a missing person or something. Yeah, a decent plan alright but tinged with fucking mentalism. He's a worry for sure.

Jones.

TUESDAY, 11th APRIL 1989
2330 HOURS
RENTED FLAT, GARNET STREET,
OVERLOOKING SHADWELL BASIN DOCK

Mate, I'm exhausted. All this raving bullshit is draining, plus, Kenny's on-and-on-and-on about getting some spending money while we wait for he rave, he's not content with the cash I'm bunging him, nor the robberies I know he's been doing with Will, the pair of twats. I've fucking told them both to calm the fuck down, they'll bring it on top before we've even started. Had a chat with Tiny too, he's on it with Devon, trying to find a sound-system big enough to cope with the venue, which is fucking massive by the way. Don't know why, just not feeling this, feels like it's going to shit.

Jones.

WEDNESDAY, 19th APRIL 1989
1055 HOURS
RENTED FLAT, GARNET STREET,
OVERLOOKING SHADWELL BASIN DOCK

Just heard from Tiny, looks like August bank holiday is favourite for the rave, thank god, might put Kenny back in his box, give him something aim for. He's still on about dealing with Devon once and for all, that he deserves nothing else after the sentence he got. To be fair, I get where he's coming from, I really do, but, we got to think about the bigger picture here, and the serious amount of cash on offer. I got to call China in a bit, see about getting the local police on board, no doubt he'll want his cut, the slippery fuck.

Jones.

FRIDAY, 21st APRIL 1989
1325 HOURS
RENTED FLAT, GARNET STREET,
OVERLOOKING SHADWELL BASIN DOCK

Just back from the gym, a monster session on the weights, then sparring with Kenny and Benji Stephens, fuck me, he can hit hard. Anyhow, Kenny came round earlier with Will, who's beginning to really fuck me off, asking to borrow my sawn-off, plans to rob a dickhead dealer in Colchester apparently. Most dealers in Essex are hooked into Bee, or, at the very least, part of Rude-Boy-Dee's connections. Turns out, this guy doesn't deal with Bee, but I thought it right to check with Dee to be sure. Calling me back, says he's not part of the Valentine crew, but, advised us to be careful, there's been loads of heat recently and he knows of at least a dozen dealers who have been picked up by the police. Goes on to say I should dump Kenny, he's a liability, reckons I should go work with him in Europe. Yeah, worth thinking about, I like the kid, he's smart. We got Millwall tomorrow, my phones been burning red with Bee, Will, The Greek, even Tiny all giving it large. My very last hooligan adventure, against our all-time adversaries, yeah, that's pretty much perfect. Bring it on.

Jones.

SUNDAY, 23rd APRIL 1989
0335 HOURS
RENTED FLAT, GARNET STREET,
OVERLOOKING SHADWELL BASIN DOCK

Millwall yesterday, at our place, dear lord. Bee sorted it like a military operation, with young kids on bikes as spotters phoning us with updates. He arranged to meet The Greek in Plaistow Park at 1100-hours, yeah, early, but the kick-off time had been brought forward to 1300-hours on police advice. Meeting Bee, Will and Kenny in Silvertown at 0900-hours, we head straight up there. The entire crew had assembled and we're all off our fucking nuts. Coked-up, fuelled by pure adrenaline, we hear "no-one-likes-us" chants in the distance followed by the unmistakable sounds of windows being put in. Soon enough, we see them, yeah, they're firmed-up like we are, roughly the same numbers too. On the instruction of Bee, we split into 3 groups of about a hundred each and charge. It's total chaos, Bee heads straight for The Greek and they begin tearing lumps out of each other, turns out, The Greek's pretty handy. Getting split up from Kenny, I see a bunch of Millwall dragging a fella away while kicking the living shit out of him. Fuck no, not Kenny. Chasing over, I take a few blows but spark-out two or three of the cunts. Up close I see it's Will, fuck, unconscious, his entire face is covered in blood. God no, what a scalp, we'll never hear the end of it. Sirens, yells and screams later, they're not backing down, neither are we. As the mounted division arrive, we all back off and, with the police helicopter hovering overhead, it's hoods on, caps down as we fade into the suburban scenery, meeting back up as planned at the Lord Stanley on St Marys Road. Reckon we could just about say we'd done them, the cunts.

Jones.

MONDAY, 24th APRIL 1989
1340 HOURS
RENTED FLAT, GARNET STREET,
OVERLOOKING SHADWELL BASIN DOCK

Just back from St Barts Hospital, seeing Will, still in intensive care, fuck me, he's in a bad way. Heavily sedated, he's got a fractured skull, broken jaw, fractured eye socket, plus his left arm and several ribs are broken, he's quite literally fucked. God only knows when he'll get out, or what state he'll be in when he does. Outside, me, Bee and Kenny agree there's no way we can ever let this go. A genuine straightener, man on man is fine, but twenty of the fucks smashing the shit out of one fella, nah, that's not right. I call The Greek, after taking the piss, he actually agrees, says it went too far, says the younger up and coming lads were to blame, he'll sort a name out for us. Bee reckons once he has it, he'll deal with him, which is just as well, I'm fucking sick and tired of all this shit, I just love West Ham. We couldn't even really celebrate our win yesterday, yeah, we fucking destroyed them 3-nill, but really, at what cost.

Jones.

SUNDAY, 14th MAY 1989
1715 HOURS
MY SECERET HOUSE, CORNER OF SECOND AVENUE AND ESPANADE, FRINTON-ON-SEA

Came over here for the Bank Holiday, mainly to get away from Kenny, says prison has changed him, and, for sure, he knows bigger words and is more academic, but, fucking hell, he's hell bent on fucking himself up, and the rest of the world while he's at it. Anyhow, had a call from China, telling me rumour's rife about the rave, as well as my involvement too. Good of him to let me know, I suppose. Says the Serious Organised Crime Unit are looking at the whole rave scene at the moment, given the large sums involved and the political interest too. Yeah, a question got asked in the Houses of Parliament during the week apparently, politicians are up in arms about the raves spreading to the gentle shires and their leafy constituencies rather than run down inner city warehouses. China says the higher-uppers suspect paramilitary involvement too, as well as high value money laundering. Asking him about Hughes, I remind him I haven't forgotten how he fucked me over, knowing he'll probably tell Hughes who'll be paranoid scared. Good, the cunt. Says he hasn't seen him for a while, but had heard he's back on the Flying Squad.

Jones.

SUNDAY, 14th MAY 1989
1715 HOURS
MY SECERET HOUSE, CORNER OF SECOND AVENUE AND ESPANADE, FRINTON-ON-SEA

Tiny called, asking for money up front to pay for the sound and lighting rig, fucking £40-grand, the cheeky cunt. I tell him in no uncertain terms to fuck right off, that's his and that arsehole Devon's responsibility, not mine, and not Kenny's. Laughing, says he expected me to say that so already has a backer in mind. So fucking what, I tell him, I don't give a flying fuck, just stop being a pussy and sort this shit out. Turns out, this backer is an old friend of Devon, fuck me, it's only "Richardson", the poncey city boy involved with Kenny being sent down. Bingo, can't believe our luck, two chop-suey twats at once. Calling Kenny straight after, he pretty much shoots his load, high-fiving himself, I could literally hear his mind clicking into overdrive. No doubt he'll be wanting to kill him too, fuck me, before we know it, we'll be wading through blood and limbs rather than counting bundles of cash. I must get back to London and calm all this shit down.

Jones.

TUESDAY, 16th MAY 1989
2340 HOURS
RENTED FLAT, GARNET STREET,
OVERLOOKING SHADWELL BASIN DOCK

Back from my secret place this morning, popped in for lunch with the folks at Bell Wharf Beach, then straight to see Kenny. Fuck me, rather than calming down, he's hyper, beyond hyper, coked-up-at-midday hyper, on about properly doing Devon and Richardson at the rave. Sniffing two to three grams of coke per day is turning his brain to dog-shit. Sure, I love a line or two but he's got to calm that shit down, way down, down to fucking china-town. It's madness.

Jones.

SATURDAY, 20th MAY 1989
2005 HOURS
RENTED FLAT, GARNET STREET,
OVERLOOKING SHADWELL BASIN DOCK

Off to a rave tonight in the midlands, a disused RAF base apparently, a few of us are going, The Greek invited us as a bit of a peace offering after what happened last month. I'm still fucking outraged about Will truth be told, but, we all know the consequences when we sign up. Tonight should be a laugh though, The Greek says he's got a public school dickhead on the books who's organising loads of raves week after week, and tonight is supposed to be the biggest so far, with around 10-thousand expected. First meeting point is Heston Services on the M25, from there, fuck knows where we'll be sent. Got my bag of coke, a dozen or so pills plus whatever Bee brings. Oh yeah, Tiny called earlier, says his financial backer, gay-boy Richardson is backing out. Learning about me and Kenny, he's running scared, the little shit, although, to be fair, he's right to be scared. Of course he's not backing out though, quite the opposite, he's fucking in, in deep too. While we don't need his money, I could fund this shit myself a thousand times over, nailing him and that cunt Devon as part of this is just an added bonus. I've suggested Kenny meets with Richardson to put him at ease, yeah, a nice candlelight dinner in a poncy restaurant in Mayfair, Richardsons choice apparently. Both me and Tiny will be there, waiting outside to ensure fair play. Safe to say, if Tiny starts, I'll end the cunt.

Jones.

TUEDAY, 23rd MAY 1989
2020 HOURS
RENTED FLAT, GARNET STREET,
OVERLOOKING SHADWELL BASIN DOCK

Sad times, West Ham are officially relegated along with Newcastle and Middlesbrough. Millwall, the fucks, finished mid-table, which makes it all the worse, a hundred times works for fucks sake. Even if we did get to the semi-final of League Cup, it doesn't count for jack-shit when we're facing the likes of dirty Leeds and shit Stoke next season. We should never have sold wonder boy Cotts, that's the issue. Plus, £2m is shit money compared to his goals, some dodgy back handers there I reckon. I'm genuinely gutted, beyond gutted actually. I love West Ham.

Jones.

FRIDAY, 26th MAY 1989
2120 HOURS
RENTED FLAT, GARNET STREET, OVERLOOKING SHADWELL BASIN DOCK

Got to look lively, meeting that old slapper Sammie in a bit, bumped into her a couple of weeks ago at a rave and we exchanged numbers. I'll take her around Soho, down a few drinks, maybe dinner, then back here for a session, yeah, fucking too right, been way too long. Anyhow, Kenny and Will, (now sort of recovered from his Millwall beating), had a successful trip to Colchester, robbing a dickhead wanna-be called John-Michael, relieving him of a duffle bag of pills, few bags of coke plus a handgun, which looks like a fucking antique from the second-world-war. Will, out of hospital for 2-weeks now, still has bruises all over and a bandage wrapped around his head and his arm in a cast, so pretty fucking easy to identify, the fucking numbskulls. Still, they also got 12-grand in cash, which is nice. Even if this guy is indeed a wanna-be prick, they got to watch their backs now, the fools. Mate, if they robbed me, I'd want fucking blood on the carpet at the very least, ideally, all my goods back too. I'll keep an ear-out for any chatter and give Rude-Boy-Dee a bell to see what he's heard.

Jones.

SUNDAY, 11th JUNE 1989
1920 HOURS
RENTED FLAT, GARNET STREET,
OVERLOOKING SHADWELL BASIN DOCK

Wow, massive come down, fuck me. Dropped maybe 6-pills last night, went to a rave near some film studios in Elstree. As promised, it was massive, the raves are definitely getting bigger, and, a lot of guys are asking me about ours at the end of August, a good sign I reckon. Listen, I love getting high, ecstasy and coke are fucking brilliant, but, I don't really enjoy these raves, don't really get it all to be honest. The music is alright, I suppose, but the whole "losing-yourself-in-the-music" is a bit beyond me, maybe I'm too old plus, I know only too well what's happening back of house and the potential for police, hooligan or gangster intervention. Anyhow, Kenny had his meet-up meal with Richardson yesterday, early evening before we headed to the rave. Reckons he's a well-groomed international piece of shit business-man with soft hands and a weak arsehole. Says he was all on not to "turn the place upside and rip the cunts heart out", (his actual words by the way). Says the dickhead got pissed-up on poncy Champagne and bought the plan hook line and sinker. The fucking idiot.

Jones.

FRIDAY, 23rd JUNE 1989
1550 HOURS
RENTED FLAT, GARNET STREET,
OVERLOOKING SHADWELL BASIN DOCK

Riding Tiny like a whores pussy, I'm checking, chasing, following-up, double-checking, calling, triple-checking and harassing him. Yeah, those two twats are lazy, unorganised fucks, real "yeah-yeah tomorrow" kind of guys, the amateur pricks. We arranged to meet at Thurrock Services to go through the plans in detail but the cunts are late, so we're left sitting there like plebs holding our dicks while sipping dishwater tea. Eventually they arrive and we go through their ideas for the rave, also promotions including radio adverts. Kenny's yep-yep-yepping away, smiling almost, but, just when I thought we were wrapping things up nicely, he suggests we go visit the venue, right there and then. Looking at Tiny, then Devon, they look scared, confused almost, but they can't refuse. Driving for about an hour, they follow in Tiny's motor while Kenny screams the shit out of his beaten up old Range Rover, (bought from Will for a grand, apparently). Eventually we get there and, holy shit, I'm blown away. Down a dirt track, up over a hill, miles from anywhere, it's literally a huge bowl of a field hidden from the main road, backing on to a forest. Fuck knows how Kenny and Will found this place, but, I have to admit, it's fucking perfect. Tiny reckons we should install a wire-fence around the perimeter to stop dickhead punters just walking in, fuck knows how though, the boundary must be at least a couple of miles. Devon, on the other hand, strolls around slowly scanning the backdrop, suggesting where we should place the stage, the lighting towers, speakers and all that. Strangely, I feel almost assured seeing these two in action. Damn.

Jones.

SATURDAY, 24th JUNE 1989
1250 HOURS
RENTED FLAT, GARNET STREET,
OVERLOOKING SHADWELL BASIN DOCK

Back from the gym, had a huge injection today. My man reckons it's called "HGH", says I'll see the results within 2 weeks. Anyhow, on the way back from the venue yesterday Kenny tells me he had a moment where he scared himself. Yeah, says he was literally seconds away from murdering those two arseholes, putting a bullet in the back of their heads, says he saw it play out in his mind. Now, that's crazy talk if you ask me, he's got demons for sure, I'll have to watch him 24/7. The last thing I need an accessory to murder charge, fuck that.

Jones.

FRIDAY, 7th JULY 1989
1755 HOURS
RENTED FLAT, GARNET STREET,
OVERLOOKING SHADWELL BASIN DOCK

Just had my old man on the phone, all passionate and militant. Yeah, says him and some old pals are thinking of protesting at the Houses of Parliament next week, something to do with the pensions of old dock workers. He asked if I could get some boys together in case it got tasty. Of course, all of us have relatives who worked in the docks, yeah, too right, I'll be there shoulder to shoulder with my old man. Saw Kenny today, says he's been thinking about Devon and Richardson, yeah, he'll make sure they come to the rave then sort them out good and proper. Says it's an eye for an eye, so, while he'll not kill them, they'll suffer serious pain. I get it, I truly do, but nothing can give him those years back, he should just move on. He don't see it like that though, of course he don't, the thick as shit lumbering fuck.

Jones.

MONDAY, 24th JULY 1989
1100 HOURS
RENTED FLAT, GARNET STREET,
OVERLOOKING SHADWELL BASIN DOCK

Another night out on Saturday, this time a fuck off massive warehouse behind Heston Services on the M4. Complete madness, but really good preparation for our rave. Me, Kenny and Will set off together planning to meet Bee there later. Will has a few deejays playing so we drive straight there, unlike the punters who'll be sent to three or four meeting spots before being directed to the rave. Getting maybe 2 or 3 miles away, the traffic's madness with punters everywhere, and there's already loads of police blocking-off roads. After a magical mystery tour, we get there a few hours later and, fuck me, there's easy 10, maybe even 15-thousand punters, all loving it, raving their tits off. The production is great, lazers, smoke machines, search lights plus, the sound-system is cracking, really-really loud. If this is the competition, then we got work to do, and when I say "we", I mean that cocksucker Devon.

Jones.

SATURDAY, 29th JULY 1989
1730 HOURS
RENTED FLAT, GARNET STREET,
OVERLOOKING SHADWELL BASIN DOCK

Got Sammie popping round later, if she eventually gets here, yeah, she's all over the place, saying she'd come mid-week, but didn't. I've got some coke, pills too, hopefully we're on for a session. Just listening to the radio, swapping between Devon's "Dream FM" and Will's "Mid-Pressure Radio", both stations are promoting the rave, giving out teasers, saying it's a "dance festival", name dropping loads of deejays and acts who'll be performing. I haven't got a clue who these dickheads are, but, it sounds impressive. Will's on board with Kennys plan to fuck those two pricks up, and, because they're up-each-others-arse-gay for each other, they think they're Einstein level geniuses. Bee's in too, providing us "close-protection" while Tiny's guys do the main venue security. Oddly, it all feels in control, which, even more oddly, makes me feel uneasy. Coppers instinct I suppose.

Jones.

FRIDAY, 4th AUGUST 1989
2310 HOURS
MY SECERET HOUSE, CORNER OF SECOND
AVENUE AND ESPANADE, FRINTON-ON-SEA

Arranged to meet China today for a long overdue chin-wag. Met him in Southend, far end of pier, which is a fucking long way out to sea. We had a good chat about the old times and how much we'd both changed. Says Hughes is still asking questions about me, like he has a hard-on for me or something. He asks if I might be interested in information on Hughes, maybe something incriminating or maybe when he might be most vulnerable. Yeah, send it my way, I smile, making sure not to seem too eager, the cunt has it coming for what he did to me. Thought I might drive up here for the weekend, think things through. Would I or could I do something to a serving officer, an ex-colleague, given half the chance. Fuck knows, suppose so, guess so, maybe. What does China get out of it though, for sure, he'll want a shit load of cash, but will that be enough, I don't want to be in his debt, or worse, he could incriminate me, the cunt. Yeah, this will take some thinking about.

Jones.

THURSDAY, 10th AUGUST 1989
2217 HOURS
RENTED FLAT, GARNET STREET,
OVERLOOKING SHADWELL BASIN DOCK

Met with Rude-Boy-Dee today, at a shit-hole called Mablethorpe, fucking miles up North, near Hull, I think he said. Fuck me, I'm getting around, a fucking 8-hour round trip. Introducing him to Kenny, we outline our plans, telling him we're expecting between maybe 20 thousand punters. Grinning, shaking his head, says we'll never get that amount, even if it was in London, let alone some fuck-off backwater in Essex. Kenny's quiet though, moody, starring daggers at him. No way I can let Kenny lose on him, I've grown to like this kid. Dee reckons we could easily punt out 5 to 10-thousand pills though, he'll do these for 40-grand, 4-quid a pill. Retailing at 10 to 15 each, that's best part of a 100-grand profit. Fuck it, Kenny grunts, we'll take 20-thousand. What the fuck. Dee looks at me, then Kenny. Yeah, I like it, okay, he smiles, all in 50-kay, that's two-and-a half a pill, cash up front. Reaching out, Kennys shakes his hand before I can say slow-the-fuck-down-speedy-fucking-Gonzalez. Fifty grand up front is serious money, still, the prospect of another 250k profit on top of the gate money is a pretty cool idea too.

Jones

TUESDAY, 15th AUGUST 1989
1644 HOURS
RENTED FLAT, GARNET STREET,
OVERLOOKING SHADWELL BASIN DOCK

Less than 2 weeks till the rave, we're mad busy with no end of shit to sort out. Kenny's got tickets printed up, just a telephone number for the phone in the Dream FM studio, and the name of the rave with a picture of a brain. "Mental Logic", they've called it, a fucking poncey name if you ask me. All the independent record shops and boutique fashion stores will take them off our hands for a fiver a go, face value is 20-quid, so they'll make a mint. I'm just surprised the punters will part with their cash without even knowing the location. Mugs.

Jones.

THURSDAY, 17th AUGUST 1989
1130 HOURS
RENTED FLAT, GARNET STREET,
OVERLOOKING SHADWELL BASIN DOCK

Back from the gym, now packing my bags. Kenny turns up with 2 plane tickets, says we're off to Marbella tomorrow to check out some villas, we'll be back on Sunday night. Bolt out of the blue, he hasn't mentioned any of this to me, but, he's so erratic right now, nothing, literally, nothing surprises me. To be fair though, a few days sun away from all this madness is no bad idea, all these pricks are getting off on the organising while all I'm looking forward to is the money, and for it to be all over.

Jones.

MONDAY, 21st AUGUST 1989
2230 HOURS
RENTED FLAT, GARNET STREET,
OVERLOOKING SHADWELL BASIN DOCK

Marbella, turns out to be a small fishing village near Fuengirola called La Cala, the very same gaff that old twat Freddie Supps, fron the Heathrow job, mentioned years ago when he attempted to bribe me. We met one of Will's buddies, "Georgios", from North West London. Tanned, gelled-back black hair, fucking full of himself, says he used to run the QPR firm but moved over here about 5-years ago. Making his name selling cannabis resin around Ladbroke Grove, he starts shipping it in wholesale via Morocco. Yeah, he had old gypsy grandmothers on the payroll swallowing 30 to 40 one-inch cellophane wrapped pellets before boarding the ferry from Tangiers to Cadiz. Demand increasing, he starts moving increasingly large amounts, firstly in small dinghy's across the Straits of Gibraltar, then in canoes with outboard motors strapped to the back. Nowadays, he uses fuck-off expensive luxury yachts, with the paid-for permission of the Major of Marbella and the local police. As a favour to Will, he has a job waiting for Kenny, running a string of nightclubs along the Costa he's in the process of buying. The following day, we're shown around a few villas by a tasty fit Scandinavian bird, all way out of Kennys price range, even if he banks what he thinks he'll bank in a weeks time at the rave. Nice to get away though, get some sun on our backs, yeah, I actually catch Kenny smiling over dinner. Surprising what the Med can make you feel like.

Señor Jones.

WEDNESDAY, 23rd AUGUST 1989
1134 HOURS
RENTED FLAT, GARNET STREET,
OVERLOOKING SHADWELL BASIN DOCK

Fuck me, all those tickets Kenny had printed up have been sold, apparently, they went in less than 2 days. Kenny wants to get another 10-thousand printed, but, the little cock-sucker Devon quite rightly says a) it's got to feel illicit and exclusive, the more tickets in circulation will ruin this vibe (his poncy words), and b), the more tickets we sell, the more likely it is the police will move in, wanting a huge pay off or locking us all up. He's spot fucking on, the twat, less is more my friend, less is more. Kenny heeds his word but is still hell-bent on fucking the prick over, Richardson too. They both got to go, so he says.

Jones.

THURSDAY, 24th AUGUST 1989
1505 HOURS
RENTED FLAT, GARNET STREET,
OVERLOOKING SHADWELL BASIN DOCK

Rest day today. Kenny came round earlier, Bee too, going over the security arrangements. Bee says we should both be tooled up, just in case. He's asked if I have any pals left in the police, maybe can I call in a favour and get the inside track, see what their plans are, or get any intel they might have on rival gangs. Sure, if I can track China down I'll ask, but I don't want to alert him by asking, nah, I'll end up being blackmailed by him, the cheap cunt. I've invited The Greek to the rave as my personal guest, mainly to ensure he's on the inside and not plotting a robbery from the outside. Says it's not for him though, reckons he's had his fill of centre-parted middle class hippy kids and funky-dred rude boys pilled out of their minds, telling him he's their long-lost best mate. Reckons Tiny has taken his core team away for a few days into the countryside for "preparation". Yeah, wall to wall raw-meat-bare-knuckle-fighting business I expect. Bee, on the other hand, is cool in the gang relaxed, says this is just like every other rave he's secured, only bigger, much bigger.

Jones.

SATURDAY, 26th AUGUST 1989
2245 HOURS
RENTED FLAT, GARNET STREET,
OVERLOOKING SHADWELL BASIN DOCK

Monday, rave day, can't come soon enough. I'm fucking shitting myself truth be told, and nah, I aint no fucking pussy, I got every reason to be concerned. Went to pick up the pills today from an associate of Dee's at Lymington, fucking miles away from London on the South Coast. The pills are imported through France to the Isle of Wight, then moved by ferry to Lymington on the mainland. Anyway, me, Kenny and Will, (Kenny's fucking bum-chum), set off early doors. At the harbour, we wait for an age before eventually a beat-up old VW Beetle parks up a few cars away and we're waved over by a young, clean cut white guy sitting in the front. Fuck me, he's the look of a deep-cover operative, shit, this is a sting, we've been set up. Swinging around, I'm looking for spotters with binoculars and van loads of armed Flying Squad fucks. Meanwhile, Kenny's leaning in through the passenger window inspecting a blue and white-ice box full of pills while Will jabs a sawn-off into the drivers face. They're fucking robbing the police, or, even worse, Rude-Boy-Dee's guy, the fucking stupid pricks. Ducking between the cars, I'm waiting for the inevitable yells of "get down-armed police", but, they don't come. Dragging him out, Will continues to point the shooter into his face as Kenny pulls out a roll of gaffer tape and tapes his wrists, pushing him into the back seat. Three blue-and-white ice-boxes in their arms, they stroll past me smiling like Cheshire fucking cats. This can't be happening, we can't rip-off Rude-Boy-Dee, or, even worse, Valentine. This is fucking bad news.

Jones.

SATURDAY, 26th AUGUST 1989
MIDNIGHT
RENTED FLAT, GARNET STREET,
OVERLOOKING SHADWELL BASIN DOCK

Been listening to Dream FM, the deejays are massively hyping the rave, yeah, there looks to be proper excitement building. Fucked if I can sleep though, been hunting around my old jackets looking for a bit of resin to help me on my way, but no luck. Anyhow, I'm called an hour ago by Rude-Boy-Dee, ranting and raving, getting all emotional, threatening to kill me and Kenny if we don't make this right. Says we're cunts for trying to rip him off and bang out of order for doing his courier pal, Ashley. Says he hasn't told Valentine yet, but will do if we don't sort this out pronto, before the rave. He can fuck right off though, I'm not being threatened by no little shit, no matter how much I like him. Kenny and Will were bang out of order, for sure, but, push comes to shove, Dee will be ended, Valentine too if they try and bring it on. Gutted, I genuinely like the kid.

Jones.

SUNDAY, 27th AUGUST 1989
0810 HOURS
RENTED FLAT, GARNET STREET,
OVERLOOKING SHADWELL BASIN DOCK

Not a wink of sleep last night, feel fucked, haven't slept right for weeks now. Setting off mid-afternoon, we're keeping a low profile until then, the only thing Kenny says he's got to do is visit Brick Lane and pick up an industrial cash counting machine. I've packed a bag with a change of clothes, just in case, along with my pistol and the sawn-off I picked up when we did Sams crack-house. Oh, even more excellent news, Kenny's arranged for a gypsy fair to arrive on site later, with a load of fighting travellers to help if things go tits up, says we'll go 50:50 with them on the take from the rides. Yeah, like fuck we will, that cash is already long gone, spent on a new caravan or two. Truth be told, it's a decent idea though, a few raves recently have had fairground rides, they look really good, memorable, iconic even.

Jones.

BANK HOLIDAY MONDAY, 28th AUGUST 1989
1004 HOURS
GYPSY CARAVAN, HALSTEAD WOODS, ESSEX

Fuck me, the toilets in these fucking caravans are pokey as hell, I can just about sit down. Even worse, I'm struggling to take a shit with the whole tribe of them right outside arguing about how much the big-wheel should cost. It's weird that I've brought you my beauty, but with my nerves, I've got to write shit down, get it out of my system and all that. We're pretty much there in terms of the final preparations, all we got left to do it a sound and lighting test by the firm Devon's hired. As well as doing security Bee's men will punt the pills, returning to the office, (a shitty 30-year old portacabin behind the stage), to drop the cash off once they have about a grand. Kenny reckons, well, Will reckons actually, the punters will all be in by 0300-hours tomorrow, so we'll count the cash after that before dealing with Devon and Richardson. I've told both Kenny and Will, in no uncertain terms, those two wankers are one thing, but, fuck with Tiny and it's literally world-war three, and we don't need that. Deep breath, this is it.

Jones.

WEDNESDAY, 30th AUGUST 1989
1440 HOURS
COLCHESTER GENERAL HOSPITAL, COLCHESTER, ESSEX

I'm here, in the very place I hoped I'd never be, avoiding the armed police standing sentry outside the intensive care unit. I haven't slept since the rave, before that actually, I'm like the walking dead. The worst night of my life starts with Devon's little brother, a well-known deejay apparently, drops a couple of pills and has a fit, writhing around on the floor, foaming at the mouth. St Johns Ambulance are on site, (an ironic stroke of genius by Devon getting them on board), and take him away, fuck knows what's happened to him. Hours later, we're counting the cash, literally piles of it actually when Devon walks in, wanting to straighten everything out. Kennys eyes change, this is it, his chance for retribution. One thing leads to another and we tape the cunt up then beat the life out of him, ends up with him telling us where Richardson is. Grassed on his old school buddy, can you believe it. Looking at Kenny, he's disgusted, after what happened to him way back when he despises snitches so goes to hack his hand off but all he ends up doing is taking best part of a finger. Devon feints then pisses himself, the sap, kind of funny to be honest. Anyhow, a few of Bee's men go fetch Richardson, they're gone about an hour but, soon as they bring him back, Kenny's on him. Punches, kicks, scratching, biting, he's like a fucking animal. Out cold, pretty much near death I reckon, I go fetch some tarpaulin from one of the gypsy caravans to wrap the cunt up and stuff him in the back of the Range Rover. Oh, hold on, police approaching...

Jones

WEDNESDAY, 30th AUGUST 1989
1530 HOURS
COLCHESTER GENERAL HOSPITAL, COLCHESTER, ESSEX

The armed officer tells me there's a commotion downstairs in reception, with a random old man demanding to see Kenny. Heading downstairs with a sub-machine gun wielding officer by my side, it dawns on me it might be Valentine, come to settle his debt, fuck. Into the reception there's an average joe, maybe 50-years old ranting and raving about seeing Kenny. Explaining who I am, he grabs hold of me and spits in my face, the dirty shit cunt. After a short scuffle, the police lead us into a side room where he tells me a god-awful tale, not sure I can actually write it down. Shit. The old mans son, Matthew, is in HMP Norwich doing a 2-year stretch for being an unwitting passenger in a stolen car. Anyhow, turns out he's hung himself, leaving a note saying he's sorry, that he loves his mum, dad and little sister, but can't live with the shame of being raped, by Kenny. Oh god, I can't write this…

Jones.

WEDNESDAY, 30th AUGUST 1989
1704 HOURS
COLCHESTER GENERAL HOSPITAL,
COLCHESTER, ESSEX

Sorry, this is so hard for me... crying his eyes out, distraught, sobbing, the old guy actually reads the letter out, saying Kenny had bummed his kid relentlessly, for months. Can't believe it, must be bullshit. I tell the guy what happened over the weekend, that Kenny might not even make it through... Nah, I can't do it, too hard, going to be sick again.

Jones.

FRIDAY, 1st SEPTEMBER 1989
1530 HOURS
KENNY'S OLD PLACE, LAUDERDALE
HEIGHTS, THE BARBICAN, LONDON

Kennys dead.

FRIDAY, 1st SEPTEMBER 1989
1645 HOURS
KENNY'S OLD PLACE, LAUDERDALE
HEIGHTS, THE BARBICAN, LONDON

Kenny's, dead. Fuck-fuck-fuck.

Jones.

FRIDAY, 1st SEPTEMBER 1989
2005 HOURS
KENNY'S OLD PLACE, LAUDERDALE
HEIGHTS, THE BARBICAN, LONDON

Fuck, first Dex, now Kenny, how will I face my mum and dad. Bee was round earlier, raging, crazy, angry, wanting revenge, wanting to kill someone, anyone to take the pain away. Tells me Will's missing too, as if this can't get any worse. Blaming Tiny, The Greek too, he's up for sorting them out once and for all, spouting everything from burning their flats down to car bombs to shotguns to cutting their heads off and spiking them on Tower Bridge. None of that's important right now. Fuck it, hearts broken, I can't believe he's gone.

Andy.

SATURDAY, 2nd SEPTEMBER 1989
1530 HOURS
KENNY'S OLD PLACE, LAUDERDALE HEIGHTS, THE BARBICAN, LONDON

Numb, like a zombie, I'm here cleaning Kenny's flat before I head to mine to do the same, then fuck knows where, maybe even Spain. Kenny, my cousin, my blood is dead. I keep replaying that night over and over, seeing Kennys face and the last time I ever saw him. Richardson's in the tarpaulin and we're crossing the meadow/car park towards Kennys motor when we hear a shout for us to stop. Looking around, there's a silhouette approaching with what looks like a balaclava on, and, from the tree-line in the woods, we see maybe four others couching towards us. Fuck. Closer, I see the balaclava guy has a rifle aimed right at us. Don't move, this need not become unpleasant, he says in a smooth Irsh accent, maybe Scottish. Fuck you cunt, Kenny shouts, dropping Richardson, before two shots pop-off and he falls to the ground too. Marched over to the motor, I'm zip-tied to the steering wheel before being coshed by a rifle butt, the fucking mugs. Waking up fuck knows how long later, the sky's a weird purple and blue colour, it's getting light with a mist hanging close to the ground. Richardson plus Kenny are gone, Bee, Tiny and most of the security guys are gone too, plus the cash, wherever the fucks that gone. Eventually, no clue where to go, ripping the zip-ties off while cutting into my wrists, I head for the hospital and find Kenny's been admitted with high velocity gunshot wounds. Fucking hell. And now he's dead.

Jones.

SUNDAY, 3rd SEPTEMBER 1989
1220 HOURS
RENTED FLAT, GARNET STREET,
OVERLOOKING SHADWELL BASIN DOCK

Can't stay at Kenny's for long, it's just too hard. I've tried making sure my prints have been cleaned and any crap belonging to me is gone. I got to go. Called China last night, asking whether there's talk about the rave, about Devon, about Richardson, about Kenny, about me, but mainly, just to talk. I ask him what my options are, maybe run off, stay and fight it out, turn queens-evidence and grass the lot of them before disappearing into witness protection. The sick fuck laughs, suggesting how funny it is I've come to him for help, reminding me I've made a lot of enemies, not just in the Met, the fucking prick. Yeah, I know his game, ham it all up so he can get a big pay-off for helping me. I've arranged to meet him tomorrow, down near the site they're clearing for the new city airport, not far from where I grew up, so we'll see. Plus, I've been summoned by Dee to meet Valentine face to face, straighten all this out once and for all. I'll arrange to meet them just before I meet China down at the airport site, all above board and nice and public, killing two-birds with one stone, so to speak. I'll pay him his 50-grand for the ripped off pills, plus some for the hassle and the distress his man must have suffered, yeah, that's classy, that'll sort it. I'm hoping by close of play tomorrow, this'll all be done and dusted and I can drift off into the shadows.

Jones.

JONES
Diary of an Undercover Psychopath

EPILOGUE

- FOOTBALL BOYS -

Dexter Bissell aka "Dex"

Tragically killed outside a South London pub in 1987, leaving a loving wife, Sue and 2 beautiful daughters. His 3-franchise car dealership business was acquired by Ruscoe-Jones Incorporated shortly thereafter, and a plaque placed on the gates of the North Bank Stand at the Boleyn Ground.

William Mallone aka "Will"

Once leader of the infamous ICB Hooligan Gang, set up one of the leading pirate radio stations across London and the South East and is believed to have organised a total of 17 illegal "rave parties". Late 1989, his security business, responsible for nightclub and shopping centre security throughout Essex was sold to Securi-Guard PLC for £7-million. More recently, he's believed to have written a dramatized screenplay of his life, optioned by Conductive Productions, London.

Byron Shann aka "Bee"

After running the East London cocaine and ecstasy distribution network through the mid to late 1980's, as well as leading the infamous ICB Hooligan Gang, wrote an award winning autobiography and has embarked on a world book signing tour. Is believed to have "retired" from all illegal activities favouring mentoring at Secondary Schools in Newham, East London. As an avid supporter, is a part-owner of a corporate hospitality box at West Ham United.

Mehmet Ahmet aka "The Greek"

Retired as head of the infamous Millwall "Buccaneers" hooligan crew in 1990, focusing instead on wholesale cocaine importation and distribution before being arrested for serious assault while on holiday on the Amalfi Coast, Italy after a disagreement about a bar bill. Deported back to the UK, he remains on remand in HMP Wandsworth awaiting trial for countless offenses ranging from grievous bodily harm to armed robbery and various drugs charges.

Claude Williamson aka "Tiny"

After a brutal war with "yardie" gangsters in 1985, resulting in life threatening injuries, built a successful security business throughout South London while earning a seat at the "top table" within the Millwall hooligan community. Along with Mehmet Ahmet, set up the largest cocaine and ecstasy distribution network in London. Late 1989, is believed to have acquired a beach bar in Saint Lucia along with long term girlfriend, Chantelle.

- POLICE CREW -

Peter Smith aka "China"

With rumours of harassment of suspects, corruption and other improprieties, controversially opted for early retirement in 1992 after unsuccessfully working a case to discover the whereabouts of a key witness to several murders within the higher echelons of London's drug distribution network.

Terry Hughes

After dismantling one of the largest drug importation and distribution businesses in the UK, as well as leading an anti-football hooligan task force, (code-named "extra-time"), mid 1993 he relocated to Lyon, France, to take up a Special Advisor role within Interpol, focusing on the drug trade between the Middle East and Northern Europe.

John Cummings

Served in various senior roles within the Metropolitan Police, featuring in a BBC fly-on-the-wall documentary "Policing London' before leaving the Met and becoming a political and social commentator.

Donnie MacDowell

Shortly after the 1981 Brixton Riots, promoted to sergeant within the Special Patrol Group. On early release from the Metropolitan Police, recruited by the Special Air Services serving a single tour in the mid-Atlantic battle group during the Falklands War. Since then, believed to be a Security Consultant to a global petroleum company in the Middle East. Current whereabouts, unknown.

- FAMILY TIES -

Kenneth McCoy

Leaving school with 3 modest exams, after a meteoric rise in the financial services sector, was arrested for possession of firearms and class-A drugs. After serving a reduced 8 year sentence for good behaviour, embarked on short lived but vicious crime spree across London, ending when he died from gunshot injuries in Colchester Hospital.

Mum and Dad
Happily settled in "The Homestead" pub and restaurant, Bell Wharf Beach, Southend until Dad contracted lung cancer in 1990, sadly passing away approximately 5 months later. After suffering a stroke, mum is now resident in Grand-Lodge Care Home, regularly receiving a bouquet of her favourite White Roses from an anonymous sender.

Janice Bevan (ex Jones)
After marrying her childhood sweetheart and cadet police officer Andrew Jones, filed for divorce in 1984. Re-marrying to David, a plumber from Hackney, she now lives in County Wicklow, Ireland, along with three beautiful children, two ponies and a Labrador named "Andy".

Claire Vaughan
After dating PC Andrew Jones on and off for several years, sold her hairdressing salon in Walthamstow before re-training as a Project Manager for a charitable organisation mentoring abused teenagers. Currently awaiting the outcome of her surprise nomination for an OBE.

Maisey Slaithworth
After a lengthy stay in Guys Hospital London with a prolapsed uterus in 1984, relocated to San Pedro, Los Angeles, where she lives with partner and film director, Bernev De-Ellacruz, believed to be a leading light in the adult entertainment sector.

Sammie Maclean

After a disastrous marriage to a British Soldier based in Cyprus, eloping with a young bartender named Christos, returned to the UK where she dated Andrew Jones before falling pregnant to a council refuse worker based in Bexleyheath, South East London. Currently happily married with two children.

- CRIMINAL FRATERNITY -

Delroy Collis aka "Rude-Boy-Dee"

Believed to be the main courier of wholesale cocaine, amphetamines, hallucinogenics and ecstasy between the UK and the Northern Europe between 1984 and 1990. Latterly, relocated to Miami Florida where he operates guided tours of Biscayne Bay.

Ben Dunning aka "Obi-Wan"

After arrest in 1985 for wholesale distribution of narcotics and various firearms offences, chose to provide witness statements under Queens Evidence, responsible for 11 custodial sentences totalling 128 years. Subject to a Police Protection Order, is believed to be living under an assumed identity somewhere in the North of England.

xxx
Bobby Love aka "Valentine"

Believed to be part of the Heathrow Bullion gang, responsible for the theft of £24-million cash and gold bullion. Went on to mastermind the largest drug network ever seen in the UK before being arrested and sentenced to an indeterminant term at Her Majesty's pleasure for murder of an off-duty Police Officer in the woodland adjacent to his estate in Kent.

Devon Walters
Having promoted the largest ever illegal rave, with an unconfirmed 30-thousand in attendance, was found dead at his flat in Greenwich, South East London a matter of weeks thereafter, leaving his beloved long term partner Shirley and son, Tyrone. The coroner officially declared the cause of death as "undetermined". Since then, several books have been written about his exploits, all of which have been optioned by Dovetail Publishing and Full-Circle Motion Pictures.

Paul Richardson
Responsible for several high profile and very profitable mergers and acquisitions in both the UK and US financial services markets, as well as serving as a Special Advisor to HM Government. Believed to have relocated to New York City late 1989 where he holds a senior position in a multinational financial services firm.

Samuel Mackenze aka "Samurai Sam"
Believed to be responsible for the introduction of crack cocaine into the UK in the early '80s. After a long battle with Yardie gangs over cocaine distribution rights in South London, relocated to Tottenham where he established the most successful drug distribution network across North London. Current whereabouts unknown, however, reports suggest he resides in Fort Lauderdale, Florida, and is working with US Federal Agents interested in several South American drug importation cells.

Benji Stephens

Discharged from the British Army after 5 and a half years, including a 3-year tour of Cyprus where he became UK Forces boxing champion holding the title for 2-years. After winning just 8 pro-fights, all by knockout, earned a shot at the WBO World Middleweight Title. He won the bout against American Dougie Harkness in Atlantic City with an 6th round stoppage.

Arry Skempell

Suspected to be responsible for the management of illicit monetary gains from several leading underworld figures, valued in the £10's of millions. Now resident in Alexandra Park Care Home, Muswell Hill, suffering from what is believed to be Alzheimer's disease, he regularly receives deliveries of Magnum 54 Cuban cigars and Courvoisier XO Cognac. Although subject to significant scrutiny by several forensic accountants deployed by the Metropolitan Police, no charges have ever been brought.

MORE FROM THE AUTHOR

The British Crime Franchise...

Book 1
"R I O T"

London, 1981. The new decade brings little hope. With one in ten unemployed and the increasing use of drugs and associated street crime blighting the inner cities, the Government adopts what's been described in the press as a hard-line approach. Newspapers and news broadcasts are filled with mass murders in the north of England, Police brutality in the inner cities and the threat of global nuclear war. The hangover from the 1970's hasn't completely worn off and, with public protests commonplace, resentment is building within the working classes. We join Devon, a part time drug-dealer looking love, his younger brother Marlon battling with rival gangs with John, a newly graduated Police constable as they duck and dive through the streets of south London. Their journeys collide on the night that changed the face of inner-city Britain for ever, the 1981 Brixton Riots...

Book 2
"R A V E R"

London, 1989. Drug dealing football hooligans, city slicker wide-boys, steroid pumped psychopathic gangsters, day glow hyper colour t-shirts and tie-dyed denim dungarees, funky dread and mid-cut curtain haircuts, love, life, babies and breakups, this is no generic gangster story; this is real life, this is 1989 and this is the UK rave scene, We follow Devon, veteran of the 1981 Brixton riots, as he descends into the murky world pirate radio, night club promotions, cocaine and ecstasy. Fate and inevitability catching up with him, he's forced to promote the biggest rave ever staged in the UK and now struggles to cope with the aftermath of the best and worst night of his life...

And introducing...
Book 4
"Y U P P I E"

New York City, 1995. The financial market and it's never-ending high-low profit-loss cycle represents a perfect symmetry and crystal-clear metaphor for what many would believe is a privileged life. I appreciate I'm erratic, one day a superstar, next day a moron, genius in the morning, retard in the afternoon and I've lived my life on nothing but my reputation. I'm not brilliant at any one thing, just slightly above average at a lot of things. Sure, for a short time, for a glimpsing moment, I was the King of Manhattan, the trader with the golden touch, mister lucky, the legendary, the one and only rock piping, coke snorting, Rolex sporting, Porsche driving, Brooklyn living, Savile Row suit wearing, earl grey tea drinking, English guy in New York, sex god of the world. Now, after getting caught, after manipulating the market, abusing my position and taking liberties, I'm literally half the man I once was, both physically and mentally. Forty years old, I look fifty, feel sixty. Yeah, I've had multiple lives packed into a single lifespan and man, I feel tired, feel like this is the end...

Printed in Great Britain
by Amazon